As winter comes and the hours of darkness overtake the light, we seek out warmth, good food and good company. But beneath the jollity and bright enchantment of the festive season, there lurks a darker mood – one that has found expression over the centuries in a host of strange and unsettling traditions and lore.

Here, Sarah Clegg takes us on a journey through midwinter to explore the lesser-known Christmas traditions, from English mummers' plays and Austrian Krampus runs, to modern pagan rituals at Stonehenge and St Lucy's night in Finland. At wassails and hoodenings and winter gatherings, attended by grinning horse skulls, snatching monsters and mysterious visitors, we discover how these traditions originated and how they changed through the centuries, and we ask ourselves: if we can't keep the darkness entirely at bay, might it be fun to let a little in?

# The Dead of Winter

# The Dead of Winter

## The Demons, Witches and Ghosts of Christmas

SARAH CLEGG

GRANTA

Granta Publications, 12 Addison Avenue, London W11 4QR
First published in Great Britain by Granta Books, 2024

A CIP catalogue record for this book is
available from the British Library.

5  7  9  10  8  6  4

ISBN 978 1 80351 153 5 (hardback)
ISBN 978 1 80351 154 2 (ebook)

Typeset in Nocturne by Patty Rennie
Printed and bound by CPI Group (UK) Ltd, Croydon, CR0 4YY

www.granta.com

*For Max, for every joyous Christmas together so far, and every one to come, and also for this one when you came with me to wassails and Krampus runs and Stonehenge solstices. I think it would be impossible to love someone more than I love you.*

# Contents

A sad tale's best for winter: I have one
Of sprites and goblins.

William Shakespeare,
*The Winter's Tale*

# The Year Walk

### 24 December

Before dawn on Christmas Eve, I slip out of the house and into a howling, windswept night, the bells of the Christmas wreath jingling wildly as I pull the front door closed behind me. I haven't spoken to anyone since midnight, I haven't looked into any fires, I haven't eaten anything. I've brought a torch with me (hoping that it doesn't count as a fire on some technicality) but I needn't have worried – behind the scudding clouds there's a bright moon, nearly full, flooding the countryside with a cold, white glow. Even in complete darkness, though, I feel like I'd know my way – I'm at my parents' house for Christmas, and these are paths I've walked since I was a child. Up to the top of the road, turn left. Past the shattered stump of the medieval wayside cross, over the drainage ditch, turn right onto the old farm track. The route is so

1

familiar, and yet this morning it feels off-kilter, shifting in the ever-changing moonlit shadows and the fierce wind that's wrenching the trees into twisted shapes. I'm walking faster than I need to, tripping in the too-large boots I've borrowed from my mother, trying not to look too hard or linger too long. I know I can't let my unease turn into fear. At best, fear might undo the magic I'm trying to invoke. At worst, it could summon something dangerous.

Once I've hopped the fence into the meadows I stop. I'm supposed to be getting far enough away from the houses that I can't hear a cock crow, and while no one keeps chickens in the village any more, I've read online that the sound carries about a mile.* This is far enough. I turn, bearing right across the fields into a little patch of woodland until I can see the village church ahead of me, the whitewashed tower a beacon in the moonlight, looming over the trees. My path puts me out at the edge of the graveyard, a dark, glittering Christmas tree just across the road. I perch on the low stone wall that rings the sprawling patch of gravestones and settle down to watch for the ghosts of next year's dead.

It was the Christmas witches who brought me here. While researching child-murdering demons with iron

---

* I'm mainly at my parents' house to fulfil the Christmas obligations of a dutiful daughter, but it did also occur to me that it wouldn't be particularly easy to get a mile away from any houses if I started from my London flat.

body parts* I ran into Perchta, a monstrous witch with an iron nose, who travels house to house every Christmas leading a cavalcade of the dead. If she finds a child who hasn't done their chores she slits open their belly, pulls out their guts, stuffs them with straw, and then sews up the wound with a ploughshare as a needle and a chain as thread. She is utterly, joyously monstrous, and when I first stumbled across her, that connection with Christmas, a time we're more likely to associate with presents, merriment and feasting than murder and dark magic, felt jarring in the extreme.

But if you look a little closer, you'll find that Christmas teems with monsters. There's Krampus, a hideous, towering demon with enormous horns who beats children with a switch or steals them away, and who rampages through Germany and Austria every 5 December. In Iceland, there's Grýla, an ogress who comes down from the mountains at Christmas and is inclined to eat her victims, popping them into a giant stew while her murderous cat – the Yule Cat – prowls at her side. In France, there's Père Fouettard – Father Whipper – a butcher who had kidnapped, murdered and tried to pickle three young boys, before he was stopped by St Nicholas. As punishment, according to the legend, he was forced to accompany St Nicholas for the rest of eternity, a looming figure lurking behind the saint, whipping children who don't deserve St Nicholas's presents. The supernatural

---

* Don't ever say I don't know how to have a good time.

dangers of Christmas aren't just limited to misbehaving children, either. There are accounts that speak of how witches were thought to be more active in midwinter, of how werewolves were more likely to turn during the Christmas period. It's a time, too, when the dead return, sometimes led by the Christmas witches in a rampaging horde, and sometimes as solemn, sad hauntings. It's a haunting I'm trying to conjure now, as I sit in the dark graveyard, the wind howling around me.

I'm on a Year Walk, or *årsgång*, a tradition that has been attested for centuries in Swedish folklore, which tells how a walk taken before dawn on Christmas Eve, without eating or drinking, without talking to anyone, without looking into a fire, will show the future. More specifically, it should show me shadowy enactments of the burials of anyone who will die in the village this coming year. It might even show me mine – there's an oft-repeated story of a man who stumbled across his own funeral procession on just such a walk as this.

Waiting in the icy darkness, the bare trees swaying violently in the wind, the church dead and empty, it feels almost believable. It's not just the night and my own jumpiness that make the morning feel strange and ominous – it's the very fact that it's Christmas, a time we've set apart, turning it into a strange, sparkling otherworld of gift-bearing visitors flying through the sky, of fairy lights glinting among trees we've dragged inside from some dark, distant forest. If magic were ever real, it would be real now. On this Christmas Eve morning I am on the cusp of the climax, the final day before the more intense

4

festivities truly begin, festivities that will culminate in the end of the old year and the beginning of the new – and new beginnings always beget omens. On top of that, the winter solstice and the longest night were just two days before: I am buried almost as deeply as I can be in darkness. No matter how much jollity we associate with the season, you can't deny that it's the perfect time for some arcane prophesying as well.[*]

And if there's any truth to the stories of the Year Walk, I need to stay alert. The future doesn't always want to be seen, and there are warnings of dangers that lurk on journeys such as these, preserved in multiple accounts held in the Swedish Folklore Archive.[†] In one version, the Year Walker loses an eye to the ghosts, in others they lose their sanity. Sometimes they simply disappear into the night, never to return. The graves in the cemetery might open, releasing those who died unhappy deaths, or a huge sow, with glowing eyes covering its entire body, might emerge to block the walker's path. Showing fear is one of the ways to summon these monsters – or stop the magic altogether. Laughter will also break the spell, and though someone might be unlikely to burst into giggles

---

[*]  In fact, prophesying death over Christmas doesn't only appear in Swedish folklore. There's also a Twelfth Night tradition in Ireland where candles are lit by each member of the household. Whoever's candle burns down first will be the first to die.

[†]  And discussed in the glorious article '"He Met His Own Funeral Procession": The Year Walk Ritual in Swedish Folk Tradition' by Tommy Kuusela, for those of us lamenting that we don't read a word of Swedish.

at the sight of an unhappy revenant or a horrifying pig, there is a Year Walk story in which two tiny, farting rats appeared in the path of the walker, causing him to laugh and forgo his chance of seeing the future. No farting rats, walking corpses, or multi-eyed sows appear in front of me this morning, but no ghostly funeral processions cross into the graveyard either.

I'm a long way into my vigil before it occurs to me that there are only a handful of burial plots left in the churchyard. Most people who die in the village will need to be buried in modern cemeteries and crematoriums, so even supposing that the Year Walk magic is working just fine, the odds of encountering a ghostly burial procession were always low. Perhaps I'll have more luck with another method – according to some versions of the folklore, if the walker circles the church three times and looks through the keyhole of the door, they'll see a premotion of a service a year from now. Anyone missing from their pew will be dead before the year is out. I slip down from my perch on the wall and walk round the church, stumbling on the uneven ground, counting the circuits,* and then I head to the little stone porch. There's a modern mesh door barring the entrance, which I expect to be locked – it normally is when the church

---

* In some versions of the story, circling the church three times will not only bring you luck in the new year but will also remove any werewolf-based curses you happen to be carrying. I don't think I was afflicted when I set out, but on this eerie, ominous night it's nice to know there's one thing less to worry about.

is closed. But to my surprise, when I pull the handle, it swings open. I duck inside, into a deeper darkness that's hidden even from the moonlight, a tinsel star hung from the ceiling swinging in the wind above my head. I give my eyes a moment to adjust to the gloom, and look for a keyhole in the ancient oak door in front of me. There isn't one. After a moment's hesitation, I reach for the latch – if the mesh door was unlocked, the main door might be too. But as I push the latch down, all I can think about is another thread of Year Walk folklore which says that every Christmas Eve, before dawn, the dead themselves hold their own church services, and they don't like it when the living try to attend – or they'll insist that the living stay. If the Year Walk magic can truly be broken by fear, this is the moment it would snap. Loath as I am to admit it, standing in that dark doorway, pushing down on the latch, feeling it give beneath my finger and start to lift, I'm afraid of what I might find waiting for me inside the church.

But the door is locked. After the initial give, the latch refuses to yield any further. I walk back outside, a little relieved, to see that the darkness is thinning, a scorched white line appearing on the horizon. I turn to head back, but take the route directly through the village rather than over the fields, keeping an eye out for any ghostly flames that should be burning where there'll be fires in the coming year. The last serious fire here was decades ago, long before I was born, so perhaps it's not surprising that I don't see any swirling, shadowy smoke hanging over anyone's homes. Year Walks, it turns out, may not be as useful

7

for predicting the dramas of modern village life as they once were. As I reach the high street, a dog walker waves at me and shouts a Christmas greeting. I feel obliged to yell one back, even if speaking to someone firmly cuts off my chance of witnessing future ghosts.[*]

There's no need for me to linger now, and besides, I'm pretty sure there are mince pies for breakfast at home. Days of Christmas cheer await, which in ordinary circumstances should shake off any idea of church services of the dead, or shadowy, ominous funeral processions. But by the time I set out on my Year Walk, I'd already met a whole host of Christmas demons. Because the more I learned of the darkness of Christmas, the more I wanted to experience it myself, to immerse myself in these terrifying traditions that seem, at first glance, to contradict the bright magic we've built around the season. This book begins on the morning of Christmas Eve, and will end on the evening of Christmas Day, but in between it will roam through the whole winter season, from murderous plays enacted in the Cotswolds on Boxing Day, to encounters with the grinning horse-skull Mari Lwyd in Wales in late January; from Krampus runs in Austria in early December and the Nordic Lussinatt festivities on 13 December (when a young woman is crowned with candles as the martyred St Lucy, who is both a beautiful, chaste Christian girl and also a rampaging witch), to the

---

[*] Sources differ on whether or not being afraid will have any effect on the Year Walk magic, but all are united in the idea that talking shatters it completely.

8

modern midwinter rituals at Stonehenge that take place on the winter solstice. This is my account of a winter spent with monsters, but it's also an effort to understand their history, where and when they originated, and why they take the forms they do.* It is an attempt as well to understand why we are so drawn to horrors at Christmastime. We may spend midwinter surrounded by warmth, good food, and companionship, but Christmas coincides with the darkest time of the year, and the legends we have repeated and adapted over the centuries remind us that beyond the glow of firelight, the shadows are waiting. Are you sure that the darkness has been kept entirely at bay? And do you think it might be fun to let a little in?

Oddly enough, the best place to start with all this isn't even Christmas. It's a little later in the winter: Carnival.

---

\* This history-understanding, incidentally, is why this book isn't a travelogue that works through the Christmas season in date order, starting with Krampus night on 5 December and finished with the Mari Lwyds in mid-January. Very irritatingly of the Christmas monsters, Krampus isn't the best way to begin if you want to peel back the layers and see where the darkness of Christmas originated.

ONE

# Lords of Misrule

*Venice Carnival*
*10 February*

It's the night of 10 February and I'm hurrying down a little side street just off the Grand Canal in Venice. A thick rain is falling, pooling on the streets, saturating the air until the entire shimmering city feels like it's being slowly submerged. It's a world of water and glittering reflections that swirl on slick stone and black canals, but I don't have time to linger and drink it all in, and it's not as if I'm dressed for a night wandering in the rain: under my coat I'm wearing a long black evening gown,[*] and covering my face is a black and gold mask

---

[*] Velvet, three-quarter-length sleeves, and a neckline my mother wouldn't approve of one bit.

piled high with jewelled feathers. It's Carnival, and I have a ball to go to.[*]

For the last two weeks, the city has hummed with celebrations. There have been boats made to look like giant rats, acrobats tumbling along the canals, fire-breathers, magicians, singers and snakes. I've spent the day wandering the city, letting drumbeats and cheering lead me to costumed dancers and stilt walkers, jesters and *commedia dell'arte* plays (where masked characters like Harlequin, the heroic, comic servant, and Pantalone, a greedy old man, act out farcical little scenes). And everywhere I go, there are sumptuous costumes – head-dresses so high and heavy that just bearing their weight is a struggle, skirts and hoops so wide their wearers have to edge sideways down the smaller streets – all of them worn with glorious, beautiful, intricate masks. In four days it will be Ash Wednesday and the fasting and solemnity of Lent will take over from the delirious anarchy of Carnival, but for now the surreal, floating city is a wonderland.

I cross another canal and wind through a set of alleyways until I reach a gate, set in a white stone wall. The

---

[*] Strictly speaking, I have the end of a ball to go to. Carnival balls are furiously, insanely expensive, and while I can stretch to the after-dinner price I don't want to bankrupt myself by buying tickets to Venetian carnival balls. Actually, that's a lie: I want more than anything to bankrupt myself by buying tickets to Venetian carnival balls – it sounds like a wonderful way to fall into a decadent and exciting ruin – but I'm begrudgingly aware that I probably shouldn't.

doorman opens it for me as I approach, ushering me into the magnificent courtyard of a fourteenth-century palazzo, and sweeping me up the stairs into the candle-lit ballroom. It's a large, rectangular space, lined by huge mirrors with *trompe l'oeil* frames and hung with enormous blown-glass chandeliers. At either end of the room are bays of diamond-leaded windows, one set overlooking the courtyard, the other facing the Rio di San Stin canal. On sunny afternoons the room must flood with golden light, but right now the little glass diamonds are sparkling black.

Not that anyone is looking out of the windows.[*] There's far too much to see inside. Winding through us are the entertainers: opera singers, magicians, a drag queen wearing giant roses on her hands, towering over the men she pulls in to dance with her, a juggler, his face painted white with black lips, desperately trying to keep his glowing, swirling balls in the air to the time of the music while the electric violinist who follows him plays faster and faster, the balls spinning and whirling ever more frantically before the music reaches its crescendo and the balls come crashing to the floor. There's a fire-eater sensually licking his flames before dragging them along his arms and over his bare chest while he writhes to the

---

[*] No one's looking at the chandeliers either. I'm desperate to know their date, but the host shrugs when I ask him and pronounces them 'very old'. Perhaps living in Venice you get used to antique glassworks that would stand up next to something by Chihuly just hanging from the ceiling.

music, dancers wearing feathered headdresses so high they brush the chandeliers, harlequins swaying on stilts – an overwhelming, chaotic, breathless display.

Even the other guests would be entertainment enough. They're wearing fantastic costumes that are loosely based on eighteenth-century fashions: huge skirts with bustles and frock coats dripping with brocades and embroidered silks. Most people have headdresses of horns or feathers (one man sitting across from me has a bird's bower on his head, with two stuffed, glistening blackbirds inside), or they're wearing traditional tricorn hats that have been covered in feathers and sparkles. And then there are the masks – laden with jewels and yet more feathers, painted and embroidered and made of a papier mâché that, softened by the heat of your body, gently moulds to your face.

The masks are fundamental to Carnival – as you walk the streets huge numbers of people are wearing them, even if they're not in any other costume. After all, Carnival is the creation of a topsy-turvy world, an overturning of the social order, and masking is part of that. When everyone is masked, identities and hierarchies are lost behind the shimmering false faces. Gender is lost as well. While shopping at a little atelier earlier in the day, I ask for a masculine mask to give as a gift and am immediately and quite rightly rebuked – masks don't have genders. Numerous costumes that I see hide their wearer's gender entirely, but explicit cross dressing is also associated with Carnival, and I encounter plenty of women wearing traditionally male outfits, and dresses worn with beards.

There's even a greeting 'Siora Maschera' – 'Ms Mask' – that can be used for anyone – man, woman, rich, poor – since anyone could be anyone behind a mask.*

The masks of Venice Carnival are associated with freedom – with everything you can do when you're anonymous and freed from the consequences of your actions. There are stories of debauchery, licentiousness and wild revelry of the kind that only comes when no one knows who you are. We know as well that people took advantage of the masks to engage in outright illegalities, including everything from challenging the government to throwing eggs filled with ink and selling pornographic images. And there were plenty of other freedoms that Venice historically allowed over Carnival, granted to anyone, masks or no. Gambling, normally illegal, was permitted, and sumptuary laws, which restricted extravagances in dress to certain ranks, were suspended (which, like the masks, also made social hierarchies harder to read – outside of Carnival you'd be able to place someone's rank by their dress alone). I'm not particularly tempted to give gambling, egg throwing or porn selling a go, but wearing a mask tonight I do feel the liberation that comes with hiding my identity. Alone at a ball I might have felt awkward, but masked I can join the crowd, anonymous and unknown, drinking and dancing with the other guests, feeling my reserve slough away.

There are darker sides to this Carnival freedom,

---

* You cannot imagine my disappointment that absolutely no one used the term to me when I was wearing my mask.

though: the idea that with everything permitted, our wildest, most unsettling desires might come to the surface; that other people might feel emboldened to do unspeakable things. And with all that, too, comes the fear that if you set the world off-balance, you might not be able to get it back into place come morning, that actions taken during a time of excess and abandon might well linger into the grey dawn that follows.

All around me, there's the press of people, the expressionless masks, the jewelled costumes, the coloured lights, the thrum of the music. It's wonderful, rich, decadent, chaotic, and then, it's too much. The effects of an entire day of glowing colour, of masks and costumes, of faces that I can't read, has left me utterly disorientated, staring around the ballroom trying to find something real to latch onto, slipping over the *trompe l'oeil*, the shifting shadows, the huge mirrors that are making it seem like this dreamscape extends to infinity. As I watch a woman in a huge, glittering ball gown fall over, drunk, to be helped back up by Pantalone and a half-naked fire dancer, the entire thing starts to feel grotesque.* The only thing I want is to get out, away from it all. I walk into the palazzo's courtyard, letting the wind bite at my skin and enjoying the ice in it, feeling the cool rain ground me. And then, slowly, I pull my coat back on, slip out of the gate and back into the empty streets.

---

\* To be clear, this comes with no judgement towards anyone who wants to get fall-down drunk in an enormous dress at a ball – after all, what else is Carnival for?

It might seem strange to begin a book about Christmas with a festival that takes place in February, but the topsy-turvy madness of Carnival may be one of our best ways of experiencing something close to our older Christmas celebrations. The chaos, the costumes, the flipping of the social order and the wild, hierarchy-shredding freedom of Carnival were all initially associated with Christmas, before they spilled forwards from midwinter to January and February and eventually became the Carnival season. For most of the last two thousand years, the days we now call Christmas were a time when you elected false kings, when you turned the world on its head and the previously impermissible was suddenly allowed. This was the uncanny foundation on which so much of our Christmas darkness grew – and I'm slightly gratified to know that I wasn't alone in finding it overwhelming as well as joyous. People had been unsettled by it for millennia.

In the mid-first century, Pliny wrote about the perfection of his villa on the coast of the Tyrrhenian Sea. Among his boasts of violet-scented terraces and a heated swimming bath he mentions his peaceful suite of rooms, and how he's especially grateful that they're well soundproofed during the festival of Saturnalia when:

> the rest of the roof resounds with cries of the holiday freedom, for I am not disturbing my household's merrymaking nor they my work.[1]

17

Saturnalia – the feast of the god Saturn – started on 17 December, and by the time Pliny was writing, it lasted for seven days and was one of the biggest celebrations of the Roman calendar. The more you read about the festivities that accompanied it, the less surprising it feels that Pliny might have wanted to hide somewhere quiet for its duration. According to his near-contemporary Seneca, it was a time when 'licence had been granted to public self-indulgence', and everyone was 'drunk and vomiting',[2] giving in to excess and luxury with wild abandon. People gave gifts, but they were often gag gifts, so that the emperor Augustus himself was apparently giving people 'nothing but hair, cloth, sponges, pokers and tongs, and other such things under misleading names of double meaning'.[3]* Normal societal rules were suspended, so that gambling, usually illegal, was allowed and hierarchies were switched and swapped, so that during the Saturnalia slaves were served a feast by their masters, and given 'licence' to speak freely. They were also allowed to recline to eat – stretching out on the long couches that were, for most of the year, the preserve of male citizens. Meanwhile men stopped wearing togas, and instead put on an item of Greek clothing called a 'synthesis' – we don't know too much about how this garment looked, but it does seem to have been colourful and it was certainly out of the ordinary. Citizens and slaves alike also

---

* The idea of going to a drunken party where the Emperor gives you a fun gift of a sponge and some of his hair makes you feel that Pliny could have sold tickets to his secluded suite of rooms.

donned a '*pilleus*' a type of cap that was normally worn only by freed slaves, so that a social status that had previously been obvious from clothing alone was, at least partially, obscured.

But if one set of hierarchies was pulled down, another one was put up in its place. Often via games of knucklebones or dice, groups of friends would elect a 'king of Saturnalia'. This king was 'absolute monarch' for the duration of the festivities, and would issue commands that their little group of subjects would have to obey, ordering their friends to do everything from shouting insulting lies about themselves to dancing naked. Even emperors played this game – Nero himself was once elected the king of Saturnalia (and used the occasion to humiliate his step-brother by forcing him to sing in front of a drunken crowd). According to Lucian, writing in the second century, Saturnalia was a time of:

> Drinking, noise and games and dice, appointing of kings and feasting of slaves, singing naked, clapping of frenzied hands, an occasional ducking of corked faces in icy water.[4]

This loss of rules and hierarchy supposedly recalled the 'golden age' of Saturn, when no one was a slave, no one held property, and 'all things were common to all',[5] a brief restoration of a time of happiness before anyone had power over anyone else. It's a lovely idea, but there's a streak of nastiness running through a lot of Saturnalia. Much of the time, the commands given by the Saturnalia kings were unpleasant – it wasn't just Nero who used them to humiliate. And of course, the real status quo was never actually abandoned. In one poem by Horace a slave speaks his mind to his master, trusting that the licence of Saturnalia will protect him, and is immediately threated with severe punishment. No laws actually protected the slaves at Saturnalia, and their mock freedoms might suddenly collapse if pushed too far. And when people in power felt free to indulge their own excesses, it often came at the expense of those lower down the social order, even if that social order should have been suspended for the festival. In Lucian's account of Saturnalia, he suggests that one of the commands issued by a king of the celebrations might be to 'carry the flute girl three times around the house'[6] – a female servant reduced to a toy to enhance the revels of free men. Watching people try to navigate the new, temporary hierarchies, seeing them attempting to work out how far they're really allowed to break taboos – and noticing that those in power, were, as always, allowed to push everything much further – you start to feel the unsettling nature of the fun, the licensed disorder with boundaries that you can't quite see until you crash up against them. Even if you disliked the status quo, even if you were glad to see it removed and overturned, the promise that it would be restored eventually lent the festival an uncertain air.

And of course, the same is true in Venice as well – no social order is really lost during Carnival. In fact, I've already classed myself as a lesser ball attendee by arriving late, by wearing an evening gown and mask rather than full costume. The balls themselves are elaborately hierarchical too, not just in payment scales but in exclusivity. If you meet someone in full costume at the Doge's Palace ball, you might not know exactly who you're talking to but it's unlikely you'll be speaking to someone too far out of your social group. It's a play at flipping the status quo, but we all know it's still bubbling beneath. And the nastiness is there as well, with some people deciding that being 'free' means it doesn't matter that they're causing harm or hurting others. I see at least two people wearing full blackface (with face paint, wigs and plastic gold chains).

The Saturnalia festival itself eventually ebbed away. We know it was still being celebrated in the fifth century, but as people converted to Christianity, belief in the god Saturn faded. By the fourth century, 25 December had been established as the date of Christ's nativity, perhaps as an attempt to commandeer the popularity of a pagan festival of sun worship at midwinter (or Saturnalia itself) and perhaps because a birthday around the winter solstice had an enormous symbolic import – Jesus as the light returning in the darkness. It also helped that a December birth meant that Jesus would have been conceived at Easter – the time of his death – giving his existence on Earth a neat symmetry. By the sixth century, the Christmas season had been set as Christmas and the Twelve Days following it – until Epiphany, or Twelfth Night, on 6 January. There were plenty of feasts in the month of December that ended up being fundamentally Christmas celebrations as well, especially St Nicholas's

Day (on 5 December) and St Lucy's Day (on 13 December). But while the mid-December Saturnalia festival was no longer observed, that didn't mean its anarchic spirit was dead – it had simply shifted, now bolting itself onto what had previously been a more formal day of celebration on 1 January or Kalends.

A century and a half before Christ, the Romans had moved their New Year's celebrations from March to January,* the date when new consuls took office. The festivities originally associated with this festival – called Kalends – were about as exciting as you'd expected for a celebration centred on politicians assuming power. In *The Fasti*, Ovid's poem about the feasts of the Roman year, he dedicates hundreds of words to the festival of Kalends† and, by his telling, people lit fires scented with saffron, wore nice clothes, and weren't supposed to argue, and if all that wasn't thrilling enough, there was also a stately procession of the new consuls to the Capitol. But the spirit of Saturnalia only had to slip forwards by a few short days to spill into the Kalends celebrations.

---

\* The vestiges of the older New Year are still visible in September, October, November and December, which were – as their names suggest – the seventh, eighth, ninth and tenth months when the year began in March.

† Heartbreakingly, Ovid left this work unfinished, so it ends in July and we never got to hear his take on Saturnalia.

By the fourth century AD, the Greek writer Libanius was describing how Kalends was a three-day festival that – like Saturnalia – revolved around gift giving, drunkenness and excessive eating, along with a shifting of normal rules and hierarchies so that slaves could be lazy, or even drunk, without punishment; rules were relaxed, and masters and slaves played dice together as they welcomed in the new year. People danced, joked, sang, and some of the more tedious individuals battered on the doors of shops to keep their owners awake all night. It was a time of riotous excess and wild fun. And while the pagan Libanius broadly approved of the festivities that attended Kalends, the Christian church was not as happy – not least because even as paganism died out, their own, Christian congregations were still causing mayhem. Until at least the eighth century, the church held that there should be a fast on the three days over New Year, a desperate attempt to rein in the merry-making, and most of the evidence for the early Kalends celebrations comes from furious Christian authors, describing in detail exactly why the festival made them so cross, and why their parishioners, otherwise fine Christians, should stop indulging in it.

In the fourth century, two of the most prolific and influential figures in the early Church, Augustine of Hippo and John Chrysostom (who was, ironically, a student of Libanius), took a firm anti-Kalends stance. Augustine called it a 'false feast day', which was, apparently, full of 'silly and disgraceful songs', not to mention 'disgraceful, junketing dances', dice playing, gift giving, and drunkenness.[7]* John Chrysostom, meanwhile, raged against its:

> all-night devilish celebrations ... the tauntings, the invectives, the nightlong dances, this ridiculous comedy.[8]

There are suggestions, too, that these 'tauntings' and 'invectives' were aimed squarely at those at the top end of the social ladder, the 'licence' of slaves to speak freely to their masters broadened, so that those on lower social rungs would also speak out against their 'superiors'. Another bishop (fifth century, this time) complained that at Kalends some people:

> make sport of the laws and the government ... For they ridicule and insult the august government.[9]

I found this ridicule of authority figures in Venice, too, where I stumbled across a jester in a little square yelling insults at the Pope to an audience of slightly baffled tourists. It's even more prominent in other Carnival celebrations around the world, and often makes a political point – in Germany in 2024 in the Cologne Carnival parade there were floats made to mock Donald Trump and the German far-right party, while the New Orleans Carnival saw parades that incorporated protests for Palestine.

---

\* Augustine doesn't specify, but I think we can assume that the gifts, gambling and drinking were all disgraceful too.

Mocking the authorities and allowing slaves to drink and play dice with their masters weren't the only ways that people were upending established norms at Kalends in Late Antiquity. From the fourth century on, churchmen also vented their fury on festive cross-dressing. One Christian council of the seventh century forbade women from dressing as men at Kalends,* and another bishop complained about how at Kalends a man might:

> loose his tunic to his ankles, twine a girdle about his breast, use a woman's sandal, put a roll of hair on his head in feminine fashion, and ply the distaff full of wool...and changing the tone of his voice utter his words in the sharper feminine treble.[10]

Complaints like these kept going for centuries, passing from angry sermon to grumpy tract, weaving their way through penitentials, being preached from pulpits and written in letters. And through it all, the general public carried on spending Kalends in wild abandon, dancing, singing, cross-dressing, 'feigning madness', drunkenly overturning the status quo, insulting the authorities and paying little to no attention to every rebuke the church issued. If anything these sorts of celebrations grew, often slipping back from Kalends into Christmas proper, and spilling forward into Twelfth Night, filling the entire

---

* Presumably they were anti this sort of thing at any other time of the year as well.

season. Until finally, in the twelfth century, the church (or at least some of its members) seems to have decided that if it couldn't beat the Kalends celebrators, perhaps it should join them. And the figure who ended up ushering some chaos into the church calendar was, surprisingly, Herod.

The 28th of December was the Feast of the Holy Innocents – the commemoration of the supposed massacre of infants by King Herod in his attempt to kill the baby Jesus. What sounds like a solemn, sombre affair had, over the centuries, turned surprisingly jovial. By the early twelfth century, there are accounts of people dressing as Herod and storming churches to throw wooden spears into the choir before slapping 'the bishop, canons and scholars' with inflatable bladders – in a manner that was all part of the actual service, and done with the approval of the bishops, canons and scholars in question. A few decades later, things took an even more chaotic turn when, in the mid-twelfth century, the Feast of Fools was established.

This new celebration seems to have started in France, and stemmed from a 1 January feast day, the Feast of Circumcision (celebrating the circumcision of Christ eight days following his birth), which had also become the day that the subdeacons – the lowest of the clerical orders – were honoured. It might well have begun in a fairly calm manner, but being on the same date as Kalends and celebrating the most junior clerics was a recipe for turning social hierarchies on their head and it wasn't long before it was all getting a bit out of hand. Despite being a part of the liturgy, despite being celebrated by members of the church, the church itself was soon complaining about it vehemently. Around fifty years after the Feast of Fools is first attested, the Pope himself was up in arms against its 'scandalous stupidities' and 'obscene revellings'.[11]

And yet, the people loved it, just as they did Kalends, and despite irritating the Pope himself, it continued to be celebrated – and to spread. By the early thirteenth century, bishops in England were complaining about it as well, furious at the misbehaviour they were witnessing.* By the fifteenth century, things were somehow even more anarchic. A letter written by the faculty of theology in the University of Paris to the prelates of France is so full of grumpiness about the nonsense that attended the feast that it's a joy to read. According to the faculty letter, the priests and clerks at the feast:

> Dance in the choir dressed as women...They sing wanton songs. They eat black puddings at the horn of the altar while the celebrant is saying mass. They play dice there. They cense with stinking smoke from the soles of old shoes. They run and leap through the church, without a blush

---

* Of course the feast couldn't have continued if plenty of the clergy didn't support it (and in England, at least, we have records of purchases for the Feast that were made by the Church).

at their own shame. Finally, they drive about the town and its theatres in shabby traps and carts; and rouse the laughter of their fellows and bystanders in infamous performances, with indecent gestures and verses that are scurrilous and unchaste.[12]

If all that wasn't shocking enough, it seems that the celebrants were even electing a 'Bishop', 'Archbishop' or 'Pope of Fools' to lead the festivities dressed in the outfit of the 'foolish' divine office, blessing people, and, all in all, profaning 'ecclesiastical dignity of hierarchical order'. Electing a leader sounds familiar – it recalls the kings of Saturnalia – but the two traditions of midwinter kings are separated by hundreds of years, and there's no suggestion of continuity between the two (and surely one of the many people complaining would have mentioned if the practice were carrying on all that time). But it was back, and back with a vengeance, an echo of the ancient celebrations that would continue down through the centuries.

And now the chaos of the Feast of Fools was spilling into the Feast of the Holy Innocents as well – and not just in the form of Herod hitting everyone with bladders. By the twelfth century, the Feast of the Holy Innocents would often involve the election of a choirboy to be 'Boy Bishop' and lead the celebrations. And while the Boy Bishop could act as a sweet, innocent child, decked out in glittering and beautiful regalia, he could also lead mischief – or worse. In England in the fourteenth century choirboys were spending the Feast of Holy Innocents throwing mud at each other during the service (after which, apparently, the entire congregation 'dissolved into laughter and illicit mirth'[13]). In the thirteenth century, in Bavaria, Boy Bishops were leading the choirboys in 'shameful games', and even arming themselves with weapons and breaking down the doors of the nearby monastery to 'treat the monks and servants of the monastery shamefully'.[14] There may well have been some exaggeration in all of these complaints, but if there is even a sliver of truth to them, then huge portions of the church had embraced the topsy-turvy nature of Christmas.

It's easy to make fun of the churchmen and their faintly prudish complaints – to see them as authority figures objecting to a festival because it involved that authority being usurped. But some elements of their fears are understandable: within these chaotic Christmas celebrations there were things let loose that could not be restrained. There were rumours of blood spilled in Notre-Dame itself during the Feast of Fools and accounts of murder during the Boy Bishop celebrations – in Salisbury in England, a member of the Boy Bishop's party was beaten to death, in Regensburg in Germany, a canon accompanying the Boy Bishop was killed, in Paris, a Boy Bishop was found dead, drowned in the Seine. When societal rules were cast aside, disorder and violence could easily follow.

Perhaps it was because of this genuine bloodshed that the complainers, eventually, had their way. It might have been all but impossible to stamp out wild Kalends celebrations outside the church, but within it, after a few centuries of complaints from bishops, archbishops and the Pope himself, the ritual was banned. In the fifteenth century, the Council of Basel, as well as dealing with the issue of the power of the Pope and the provision of military assistance against the Ottoman Empire, also outlawed the Feast of Fools. The feast lingered for a while, but was helped into its decline (across some parts of Europe) by the coming Protestant Reformation, which took an extremely dim view of the entire business, and largely crushed it. On the secular side, though, things continued apace. After all, the church had tried to ban Kalends celebrations outside of its walls plenty of times before and had never yet succeeded.

Although the church might have wished for the Twelve Days of Christmas to be entirely devoted to a celebration of Christ, the unruly mayhem continued, with its highpoint often coming on Epiphany or Twelfth Night (hence Shakespeare's play of the same name, which is full of drinking, pranks and cross-dressing). And a new practice was emerging – or, at least, an old one in a slightly different guise. Starting in the late medieval period, the kings of France had begun electing their own Christmas rulers to preside over the celebrations – the kings of Saturnalia and the Popes of Fools made anew, but with a twist. These new Christmas kings were elected not by casting lots or elections, but by baking a cake with a bean hidden inside. Whoever found the bean in their slice was king for the length of the festivities. This game was picked up by English monarchs in the fourteenth century,* where the cake-ordained ruler was often known as the Lord of Misrule. And it wasn't just the monarchy who engaged in these elections. Cities, schools, colleges, royal and aristocratic households all elected their own Lords of Misrule, Abbots of Unreason, Kings of the Bean, Kings of Christmas and Lord Balthazars.

The celebrations they led could be as unrestrained and excessive as those overseen by the Popes of Fools and Boy Bishops. There are accounts of Lords of Misrule playing pranks, running (uninvited) into church services dressed in motley, and conducting mock religious rites. In the seventeenth century, the puritan pamphleteer Philip Stubbs was furious about the Lords of Misrule, and the 'devilry, whoredom, drunkenness, pride and whatnot' that these 'fantastical fools' brought with them.[15]

---

\* In the terrible Netflix Christmas film *A Knight Before Christmas*, a time-travelling English knight comes to modern-day American from 1334 and introduces Vanessa Hudgens to the practice of hiding a bean in a cake at Christmastime, a custom that – to him – must have felt fairly modern, with its first recorded incidence in England happening only twenty years before. Perhaps this is why he gets it wrong, and tells her that finding the bean means she can have a magic Christmas wish, rather than being crowned queen of chaotic revels (this is the kind of fascinating insight into Christmas traditions that you won't find outside of this book).

When Robert Dudley, the favourite of Queen Elizabeth, was elected as a Christmas Prince by the Inner Temple (a professional body for lawyers and judges), he led a hunt of a fox and a cat around their great hall on Boxing Day night, the animals torn apart by a pack of hounds under the wood panelling and illustrious portraits. There are accounts, too, of Lords of Misrule breaking down doors, smashing windows and leading riots. One Lord of Misrule was even tried for manslaughter in England after his Christmas games went awry. The status quo might be awful – it might even be profoundly evil – but throwing it off and giving in to wild abandon brought dangers of its own.

The anarchy of Christmas continued outside of the Lords of Misrule as well – Increase Mather (the American clergyman who brought his deranged unpleasantness to the Salem witch trials) claimed that Christmas was spent 'in playing at cards, in revellings, in excess of wine, in mad mirth',[16] and even compared it to Saturnalia, while Philip Stubbs complained that:

> More mischief is that time committed than in all the year besides ... What dicing and carding, what eating and drinking ... to the great dishonour of God and the impoverishing of the realm.[17]

In England, Parliament under Oliver Cromwell even tried to ban the festivities altogether, an attempt that lead to Christmas riots as people took to the streets in protest.

In the end, what put a stop to the Christmas madness wasn't a ban, but the rise of a compelling alternative vision of the festive period. In the Victorian era, the wildness of Christmas wasn't just tamed – it became thoroughly domesticated. The new fashion for Christmas celebrations embraced the festivities, the good cheer and the parties, but also set them firmly inside the home. Family was becoming central to Christmas, with Queen Victoria and Prince Albert portraying themselves celebrating in domestic bliss, surrounded by their children. Charles Dickens, meanwhile, was publishing *A Christmas Carol*, which also pushed a family-based Christmas, whether it consisted of roasting a goose and going to church with your children or playing parlour games round the fire with relatives. This new Christmas caught on, helped by the fact that the holidays had been enormously constrained by urbanisation and industrialisation. Most workers didn't have a week to celebrate any more, but only a single day (think of Bob Cratchit begging Scrooge to have Christmas off – even with that granted, getting to church and eating a festive dinner didn't leave him much time for any Christmas mayhem). And while the new Christmas was still centred on celebration and merry-making, it would no longer turn the world upside down. If anything, the status quo would be reinforced – the master of the household at the head of his table, the queen and her consort in their palace, and a complete absence of riotous disorder.

The tradition of Christmas Kings still survived in England, but in the quietest way possible – the bean in the cake becoming a coin in the Christmas pudding, and a vague idea of 'luck' being attached to whoever found the little token in their slice. In France and Germany, meanwhile, there was still the King Cake, with a little porcelain figure of the infant Jesus baked inside to be discovered by the king or queen of the celebration* – but as the family Christmas caught on beyond England the kings and queens stopped leading disruptive celebrations and simply each wore a paper crown.

But the wild energy of Christmas had slipped elsewhere in the medieval period, and here it survived right down to the present day. We have hints of where it went just through the cakes. In Louisiana, the traditional King Cake is thought to have been brought over by European settlers in the eighteenth or nineteenth centuries. A little figure of Jesus is hidden inside, and the one who finds it is made king or queen for the day (and is responsible for buying the cake the next year). But this cake is associated not with the period from Christmas until Twelfth Night, but from Twelfth Night until Shrove Tuesday – that is, the period of Carnival, a festival that had started to grow in the thirteenth century.

For much of the early medieval period, Christmas was often regarded as the opposition to Lent – a time of wild revelry before the restraint and piety that started on Ash Wednesday and ran until Easter. Carnival,

---

\* The figure is still called a 'feve' – a bean – a reminder of its previous form.

meanwhile, was nowhere to be seen. It the twelfth century, the most excitement to be had in the pre-Lent, post-Christmas period was the Pope piously witnessing the slaughter of some animals on the Sunday before Lent. These creatures were linked with various sins (a bull for pride, a cock for lechery, and a bear for the devil) that should be similarly destroyed so that people could 'be counted worthy to taste the body of the Lord at Easter'. It wasn't until the thirteenth century that the mayhem we associate with Carnival began to emerge, and all of it seemed to be borrowed from Christmas – an expansion of the wild Christmas revels, filling the space between Twelfth Night and Lent. By the early modern period, Carnival could even start on Boxing Day (in Venice, masks could be worn from the 26th onwards) – a near complete overlap of the two festivals. By the fifteenth century, there were clerical complaints about all those who:

> danced on Ash Wednesday … and all men who have dressed in women's, monks or priests' clothes, or women who have disguised themselves in men's clothing … performing plays, japes or rhymes in scorn and despite of priests, confessors, or any holy Christian thing.[18]

Here is a continuation of the chaos of Kalends, shifted down through the year. Christmas and Carnival would stay connected – one bleeding into the other, Carnival taking more inspiration from new Christmas revelry,

and Christmas stealing back traditions from Carnival.[*]
There were plenty of other traditions that helped form
Carnival as we know it today – especially as it developed
in America – but when I participate in the wild abandon
of Venice on 10 February I am seeing a little piece of the
anarchy of our old Christmases.

As I walk back through Venice after the ball there's an
eerie quiet hanging over the city. The only sounds are
the falling of the rain, the little streams running down
the gutters, the splashing of the canals lapping against
their stone banks. There are still some masked revellers
wandering the streets, but they're silent, heads bowed
against the rain, drifting through the city. As I cross
a canal just past the Rialto Bridge, I see a figure in the
shadows. They're wearing a black hooded cape, a tricorn
hat, and a bauta – a white full-face mask that flares out
at the chin. It's one of the earliest attested Carnival costumes known in Venice, and one of the most unsettling,
the face entirely covered but given an unnatural shape,

---

[*]  We'll come across plenty of these Christmas/Carnival swaps, but
one of my favourites is the 1999 erotic thriller about masked misbehaviour, *Eyes Wide Shut*. It was based on a book – *Dream Story*
– that was set in Vienna during Carnival, but Kubrick transposed
the action to a New York Christmas, turning it into an unsettling
otherworld of glimmering fairy lights. Now that the 'Is *Die Hard* a
Christmas movie?' argument has fully died down, it's time to start
the 'Is *Eyes Wide Shut* a Christmas movie?' discussion. It certainly
has the potential for making the post-turkey entertainment with
your family a lot more interesting.

the eyes shadowed so they're two black pools staring back at you. It's not a coincidence that the word for a Carnival mask – 'larva' – also translates as 'ghost'. Seeing the figure lingering in the darkness, in that silent, empty night, the white face glowing in the street light, feels like a haunting.

By the time I get back to my hotel, I'm unsettled, damp and desperately in need of a reassuring hot tea. But if you think the older, darker side of Christmas can be avoided by staying away from Carnival, think again. Carnival is only one of several winter celebrations that came to channel some of the old midwinter chaos. And while Carnival grew into a surreal dreamscape, these other Christmas traditions shifted into nightmares. Masks were associated with Kalends from at least the fourth century on, but they don't look anything like the ones I see at the Venice Carnival, in all their glittering wonder. Instead, they were the masks of monsters. And to find these monsters – and meet them in person – I need to go to back to England, to the south-west and a little village nestled in the Cotswolds, on Boxing Day.

TWO

# Monstrous Visitors

*The Marshfield Mummers Play*
*26 December*

I'm standing in a small crowd on the high street of the
Gloucestershire village of Marshfield, waiting for monsters. After the glittering excitement of Christmas Day
– the food, the drink, the gifts – Boxing Day morning has a
flat, empty feeling. The weather is grey and drizzly, which
matches the setting perfectly: a jumble of grey stone
houses, most of them centuries old, line the grey street,
which is dotted here and there with bare, grey trees. We're
singing Christmas carols, but no one's heart seems to be
in it. Two elderly women behind me complain that they
have hangovers from the day before;* a bored child kicks

---

* They also have some strong opinions on the calibre of the judging
  in the annual Marshfield Christmas wreath competition.

the ground listlessly. On my drive down earlier today the roads, never bustling, were entirely deserted.

We're in the *Internächte* now – the 'in-between nights' – a term used in some areas of Germany and Austria for the period that runs from Christmas Day to Twelfth Night, on 6 January. It's a good word to describe the strange, quiet interval that follows the chaos of Christmas itself and runs (at least in modern times) until New Year; a period when you lose track of time, as the normal working week is, for many people, suspended. Throughout history, this period has been associated more with relentless feasting and festivities than the quiet of the modern day, but it was still an in-between time, when nothing was quite as it should be – a perfect moment for the supernatural to slip through. In Marshfield, it's what we're waiting for.

The village clock strikes 11 a.m., and the crowd on the high street abandons the carol singing, staring up the road expectantly. As the striking finishes, another bell picks up, and a strange, shuffling group makes their way towards us, led by a town crier in a top hat swinging a handbell. The five figures following him are wearing huge, bulky outfits made from strips of paper, covering their bodies like shaggy animal hides. They have a hulking presence – looming and animalistic – their faces covered by more paper shreds that hang down from their hats. When the wind catches the strips, you can sometimes make out the human mouths beneath them. They are profoundly unsettling figures, shambling behind the bell-ringer, who forms them into a circle in front of the crowd.

First to step into the centre and speak is the most disturbing figure of the group, wearing a peaked red hood hung with strips of red paper, obscuring his face – a blood-red Grim Reaper who intones in a flat, solemn voice:

> In comes I, Old Father Christmas.
> Christmas or Christmas not,
> I hope that Father Christmas shall never be forgot.

The last line has the ring of a threat; Santa has never seemed less jolly.

What follows is a bizarre play acted out by the paper-covered figures, in which Little Man John is slain by King William, only to be brought back to life by a doctor, after which Beelzebub solicits money from the audience. In all, it takes about six minutes, and is delivered with utmost solemnity, the lines chanted in a sing-song monotone. Even when Dr Finnix touches a character's legs and announces, in deliberate innuendo, that he can 'feel something hard' the inflection doesn't change. The audience gets involved as well – we boo as Little Man John is killed and cheer when he's resurrected, but the reactions are muted, almost scripted. It's less like an expression of real emotion, and more like we're playing our own part in the drama, participating in a ritual that we don't fully understand – a disconcerting experience at the best of times, let alone when the ritual in question features death and the devil, and is acted by shuffling, faceless monsters.

As the play finishes, the performers parade in a circle, singing tunelessly. The town crier rings his bell again and they lumber off, but the crowd follows – the players aren't done yet. Perhaps a hundred yards down the road, in front of a row of grey seventeenth-century almshouses, they come to a halt and the whole performance starts again. Old Father Christmas re-introduces the play. John is stabbed again, the crowd boo again, he's resurrected, the crowd cheer once more. The town crier leads us further down the high street, and there's yet another performance. In the grim, monotonous repetition, the play becomes even more surreal. It feels like we're building towards some unknown climax.

There's still one more performance to go, in front of the pub. As the players finish the landlord comes outside to offer them whisky and they raise their glasses, downing their drinks together. One cheers and takes off his hat, revealing a perfectly normal man beneath, and the spell abruptly shatters. There is genuine laughter and cheering from the audience, and we all pile into the bustling, noisy warmth of the pub.

This performance is not limited to Marshfield – it's part of a centuries-old Christmas tradition known as mumming (or mummering). Some parts of the Marshfield play are unique, but the structure of it – the death, the resurrection by a doctor, the pleas for donations, the inclusion of Beelzebub and Father Christmas – is found in similar performances all over Britain, an echoing of strange, murderous, devil-filled plays that fills the country at Christmas.

In the performance in Ashdown in Sussex, it's St George who fights a Turkish Knight instead of King William fighting Little Man John. The Christmas play in London on Bankside uses the same names, as does the one in St Albans. Elsewhere in the Cotswolds there's a variant play with Robin Hood; in Scotland the St George character is called Galoshin. Sometimes, the murderer is simply called 'Slasher'. In some Irish variants, it's St Patrick against the evil Oliver Cromwell. Beelzebub hops through the majority of them, collecting money from the audience, Father Christmas almost always announces the proceedings, and in most cases the victim is revived by a doctor. Most of these plays are significantly merrier than the one in Marshfield – instead of solemn intonations there's genuine shouting, cheering and laughter from the performers.* The costumes change as well – often the players dress as their characters, St George wearing a cheap Crusading-knight costume from Amazon; Robin Hood in a feathered hat and holding a bow and arrow.† But they

---

* Marshfield has one of the most sombre mummers plays going, quite possibly because it was revived in the 1930s by an over-enthusiastic folklorist who impressed on the performers the idea that it was a sacred ritual and so needed to be treated seriously.

† Inevitably, the Turkish Knight tends to be a horrible amalgamation of racist tropes (and is often portrayed by someone with a blacked-up face). I cannot imagine what goes through the minds of those deciding that the parts of past that they want to preserve and rehearse and rehash year after year are racism, prejudice and bigotry.

are all, to a one, disturbing to watch, dancing with devils and centring on Slashers and murderers, and all of them have the feel of a ritual that taps into something utterly ancient, something with a profound significance that is now all but lost.

I'm desperate to understand what I've participated in, and I'm surprised (and a little disappointed) to discover that rather than being an arcane mystery, or a folklore that has been passed down through the ages, we can actually pinpoint the origin of the plays fairly easily.

A few months after Marshfield, I'm sitting in the Rare Books and Music Room of the British Library with a yellowing pamphlet on the desk in front of me. It's poorly printed and badly cut, the edges of the pages slanting and sitting slightly askew. Surrounded by leather-bound, gilded volumes it feels like a miracle that this little scrap of a book has survived 300 years. The title page reads *Alexander and the King of Egypt: A Mock Play as is Acted By the Mummers Every Christmas*. It records a play in which Alexander fights Prince George, son of the King of Egypt. George is wounded in the fight, at which point he is cured by a doctor. There is a final scene tacked onto the end, where George fights and kills his father (who remains firmly dead) but the similarities with the modern mumming performances are clear. Here, we are seeing what all the death and resurrection in the modern plays developed from – a story about a doctor who cures a wounded man, rather than bringing a dead one back to life. For all its feel of the archaic, the structure of the Marshfield play dates to the eighteenth century. Little books like the one in front of me may be why this particular type of play became so widespread. *Alexander* reprinted frequently, and other cheap pamphlets (commonly known as chapbooks) reproduced their own variants. Carried on cheap, rough paper, the stories were disseminated throughout the country, inspiring groups into their own performances, even while the mummers added bits and pieces of local tradition. The chapbooks account for the similarity of the plays across England – writing fossilises things, helping them spread while keeping them relatively unchanged.*

The plays might seem strange to us now, but positioned in the mid-1700s they become a lot easier to understand – they feature stock characters passed down from Tudor and Stuart dramas, and worked off stories that had been popularised by earlier chapbooks (Richard Johnson's 1586 *Seven Champions of Christendom*, for example, was likely responsible for the introduction of St George). Sometimes they cribbed off other common literature of the time – *Alexander* quotes lines from a popular song called 'The Infallible Doctor', which has led to suggestions that the entire character of the Doctor might come from this seventeenth-century ballad about a travelling quack (although it has to be admitted that

---

* Chapbooks were responsible for spreading a lot of other traditional stories as well. When Perrault, for example, wrote his version of *Cinderella* in France in 1687, his additions to the story (especially the pumpkin transformed into a coach and rats turned into footmen) spread to England through chapbooks, which had such influence that these elements became built into most English tellings.

travelling quack doctors were a staple of comedy across the UK and Europe at the time). These plays only feel to us like lost rituals because we've forgotten what shaped them in the first place.*

But despite this fairly mundane explanation for the mummers' performances, there are still things lurking within them that speak to an older darkness at Christmas. For a start, the tradition of murderous, devilish Christmas plays long predates the seventeenth century, and is found across Europe. These plays particularly stemmed from 'mystery plays' – performances that were originally put on by the church to help communicate stories from the Bible, but that passed into the hands of town guilds in the thirteenth century after a papal edict forbade the clergy from acting in them. The guild plays still focused on Bible stories, but they tended to be jazzed up for the audience, and leaned hard into melodrama and spectacle. They also tended to be performed at festivals through the Christian calendar, and the ones at Christmas could be especially gory. The 28 December play for Holy Innocents Day was a firm Christmas favourite. Herod would appear with babies skewered on lances, laughing about his evil deeds, his soldiers throwing

---

* Imagine a twenty-first-century pantomime, performed almost unchanged centuries later, littered with references to current events and popular culture that have now been forgotten, with 'it's behind you' chanted solemnly and seriously by the audience, none of whom have any real idea why – for this one type of play – they're obliged to shout a ritualised warning at the characters, in a way they'd never do in any other performance.

around prop babies and boasting of the bloody murders they'd committed. One German performance even had blood-filled wooden dolls that could be impaled and torn apart for maximum effect. Herod would often be dragged to hell by devils at the end of the play – in one case, he was flown there, maggot-eaten, seated on a throne. Such was the expectation that Herod would be an utterly scenery-chewing villain that in Shakespeare's *Hamlet* the prince advises his actors to not 'out-Herod Herod' – that is, not to vastly overact – when they perform. Even if the play were a Nativity play, devils still appeared – in one thirteenth-century version, Lucifer himself tries to per-suade the shepherds that the angel has lied to them, and that their faith is misplaced. These devils and demons were the highlight of mystery plays – a chance for excitement and pyrotechnics. In one fifteenth-century performance, a devil had 'gun powder burning in pipes in his hands and in his ears and in his arse'.* In other cases, Hellmouths blazed with fire and cannons, and opened on their own accord. People liked the devils, and the mas-sacring, overacting arch-demon Herod, and they became a staple of Christmas celebrations. A Christmas play without a devil was hardly a Christmas play at all. The one Beelzebub and single (undone) murder of Marshfield starts to feel a little tame in comparison.

---

* I'm starting the petition here for school Nativity plays to include fire-farting devils.

But there are other monsters in the Marshfield mumming beside the murderous king and the Devil. After all, while the costumes gesture vaguely towards the characters – William wears a paper crown, Father Christmas is all in red – the main purpose of the outfits seem to be to entirely disguise the players, making them unrecognisable as people and giving them the uncanny impression of being monsters who have decided to put on a performance. This is because the play came second, laid over an older tradition that revolved around dressing as monsters at Christmastime.

Another element of this earlier tradition is still visible in the bizarre repetition of the play through the village, a fossilised remnant of a time when monsters would go from house to house, parading through the town, knocking on doors and demanding to be let in.[*] Once they were inside, they'd insist on being given food, drink or money

---

[*] The reason this sounds an awful lot like trick-or-treating is because the two are related. However, it's a sign of how much Christmas spookiness we've lost that it feels genuinely surprising to discover that it was originally a Christmas custom that later spread to Halloween. In the Middle Ages, 'Souling' on Halloween was traditional – a ritual begging where people knocked on houses promising to pray for souls if they were given 'soul cakes' – but the terrifying costumes were added later, and seem to have slipped back into the season from Christmas. All of this house visiting may also have been the origin of our door-to-door carol singing, and the practice of first-footing, in Scotland, Northern England and the Isle of Man, where the first person to enter the house on New Year's Day is considered a bringer of good luck and should be given food or drink by the householders.

before they would leave.* The play – whether it was the story about the death and resurrection of Little Man John or something else – was added later, something for the monsters to do once they got inside. This earlier tradition of going door to door has numerous different names (including, unhelpfully, mumming), but the most common one (and the one I'll be using here) is 'guising'.†

Unlike the death-and-resurrection mummers play, dated so securely (and so disappointingly) to the eight-eenth century, Christmas guising is over 1,500 years old: wearing costumes and masks was associated with Kalends from at least Late Antiquity. Alongside the clergy complaining about topsy-turvy social disorder, they were just as many bemoaning that people were dressing up and going from door to door demanding food, drink and money. In the mid-fourth century AD, Bishop Ambrose of Milan recorded a tradition 'of the common people', where on 1 January they disguised themselves as stags. His con-temporary, Bishop Pacian of Barcelona, wrote a short

---

\*    This tradition, by the way, may be preserved in the song 'We Wish You a Merry Christmas', in which the singers demand figgy pudding and say that they 'won't go until we've got some'.

†    This blurring of the names muddies the waters enormously if we want to understand just when guisers started performing plays. When, for example, Edward I had 'mummers' at his daughter's Christmas wedding, were they gusiers or guisers giving a play? It's impossible to tell – although it does seem there was a period in the Middle Ages when guisers/mummers played dice games rather than giving plays. The first mummers plays we have recorded, though, are those in the eighteenth century.

treatise condemning the act (called *Cervus* – 'stags'). The treatise hasn't survived, but we do have Pacian's rueful (and endearing) musing that many people who hadn't previously known about the practice had read his treatise, thought dressing as a stag on 1 January sounded quite fun, and started doing it themselves. 'I think,' he reflected, 'that they would not have known how to make themselves into stags unless I had shown them by reprimanding them.'[1]

At the very least, Pacian's treatise doesn't seem to have stopped anyone – a hundred and fifty years or so later, in Arles in France, Bishop Caesarius gave a New Year's sermon in which he furiously complained about men who went about on the first day of January dressed as 'a little stag, a heifer, or any other kind of monster'. In another New Year's sermon, the bishop was just as cross about people who on 1 January 'want to transform themselves into the condition of wild beasts'. In the ninth century, he was echoed by another penitential which insisted that if anyone on 1 January:

> goes about as a stag or a bull; that is, making himself into a wild animal and dressing in the skin of a herd animal, and putting on the heads of beasts; those who in such wise transform themselves into the appearance of a wild animal: [they must do] penance for three years because it is devilish.[2]

And while calling these stags 'devilish' was just a way of calling the entire business of guising an unsuitable practice for good Christians, there are hints that the disguises were intended to be unnerving. According to Chrysologos, the guisers also blackened their faces with charcoal and:

> so that their appearance may reach the level of utter and complete terror, straw, skins, rags, and dung are procured from all over the world, and anything connected with human shame is put on their face.[3]

This disguising blended as well with all the cross-dressing associated with Kalends, so that Chrysologos could also be furious that these celebrants 'turned men into women'. And the guisers weren't just dressing up – they were also going from house to house, demanding gifts. Bishop Caesarius insisted that his congregation should not allow these monsters to 'come before your homes' (which, of course, suggests that coming before their homes was exactly what the monsters were doing). Meanwhile, Chrysologos claimed, appalled, that the guisers were 'what Christians look forward to, what they allow into their homes, what Christians welcome in their homes.'[4] Asterius, a writer in the fourth century BC was just as furious about the 'squads and hordes' that:

> hang about every house ... the gates of public officials they besiege with especial persistence, actually shouting and clapping their hands until he that is beleaguered within, exhausted, throws

out to them whatever money he has and even what is not his own. And these mendicants going from door to door follow after one another, and, until late in the evening, there is no relief from this nuisance.[5]

But, as with all the Kalends complaining, no one seems to have listened – in AD 1020, the Bishop of Worms was still crossly asking, 'Hast thou done anything like what the pagans did, and still do on the first of January, in the guise of a stag or a calf?'[6]

But if this tradition of going house to house dressed as monsters – and, specifically, horned monsters – was well established in the Middle Ages, and first appears in the sources in Late Antiquity, where did it come from? It seems unlikely that it sprang up fully formed in the fourth century, and nothing like it is attested in any of the Roman festivities of Saturnalia (or the Roman Kalends).* This leaves the suggestion that it might have existed as a tradition in Europe outside of Rome, prior to the advent of Christianity. Now, this is a suggestion that requires a very firm hand because before the fourth century and the Bishop of Milan, we have no sources whatsoever for monstrous guising. The lack of sources doesn't rule out the idea that it was a pre-Christian European tradition – we don't have much of idea about

---

* There is one image relating to Saturnalia that does show a mask, but it's a stage mask of a human face, with no antlers or animals involved.

the bulk of pre-Christian European beliefs,[*] so it's perfectly plausible that it was going on. But without written evidence there's very little we can actually say about it that's not utterly unhelpful guesswork. Perhaps it was the survival of an animal cult that was attached to midwinter. Maybe it was never a religious thing, and the pre-Christian religious authorities of early Europe hated it just as much as the later priests and bishops would. Maybe it was invented in the year before the Bishop of Milan wrote about it.[†] Maybe it was already millennia old by the time he put pen to paper. If you really want to play games, maybe it was all made up by Pacian, and, as he feared, everyone learnt it from his book. You can guess away, but it will only ever be guesses. Following the tradition back as far as it can go and then watching it slip into unknowable darkness is almost as disappointing as discovering that the English death and resurrection mummers plays are only 300 years old. But if we don't

---

[*] There are, for example, only a handful of mentions of Druids in Roman sources – and none anywhere else – and it seems likely that they were the religious leaders of Northern Europe. If we only have a few sentences on them, it's hardly surprising that we have nothing on guising.

[†] This might sound like I'm being facetious (probably because I am being, at least a little), but traditions, rites and rituals are invented all the time. They have to spring up somewhere, after all. Never mistake folklore for something ancient and unvarying – it is creative and dynamic, ever changing. Someone, on some 1 January, was the first person to don an animal mask and run around from house to house, and there's no reason why that someone couldn't have lived in the fourth century AD.

know where it came from, we can certainly follow where it went.

By the later Middle Ages, guising isn't just referenced by angry churchmen. In 1263, in Troyes a practice called *'momment'* was recorded as a Christmas activity – likely a word derived from the Greek word for mask *'mommo'*, and suggestive of guising. In 1348, people in the court of Edward III dressed up as animals over Christmas. In the earliest sources from Iceland, meanwhile – that is, in the mid-thirteenth century – there are hints of a house-visiting tradition featuring men dressed as the ogress Grýla. Even Bishops started to get in on the fun – in 1406, the Bishop of Salisbury enjoyed 'disguisings' in his manor during the Twelve Days of Christmas. The Boy Bishops, as well, went door to door demanding treats, mirroring the actions of the guisers even if they weren't dressed as monsters themselves.

Christmas guising may even lie at the heart of one of the best-known medieval poems – *Gawain and the Green Knight*. The opening of the poem takes place during the Christmas celebrations of King Arthur's court. Amid the feasting and merrymaking, a terrible, bizarre figure comes through the gates – a giant man, entirely green and riding a green horse, carrying a stick of holly in one hand and an axe in the other. He has come, he says, for a Christmas game. Any man can strike him with his axe, on the condition that a year and a day hence the blow will be returned. Gawain accepts the challenge, and, thinking to avoid receiving any blow in return, beheads the Green Knight. But the knight – horrifyingly – does not fall even as his head rolls across the floor. Instead, he reaches out with his enormous hand, picks his head back up again, mounts his horse, and reminds Gawain that in a year and a day the blow will be returned. As he rides off, as the court sits in silence, as Gawain contemplates the fact that the returned blow he must submit himself to will surely kill him, Arthur declares that this is exactly the sort of thing one might expect at Christmas.

To modern ears this is a baffling claim, but in an age where monsters might well come knocking at your door over Christmas time, perhaps even proposing games or plays, Arthur's statement rings true. More to the point, the Green Knight is a man in disguise (not that Arthur knows it). When Gawain reaches his appointed meeting place with the knight a year and a day on, he finds himself hosted by a lord, Bertilak de Hautdesert. Gawain eventually bends his neck to the knight to receive his blow (which barely nicks his skin) at which point the knight laughingly reveals that he is, in fact, Bertilak, magically made to appear enormous and green.

Oddly enough, the most jarring part of the poem – the blow-for-blow promise, the beheading, and then the chilling moment when the knight picks his own head back up off the floor – is a surprisingly common set piece in Irish and French literature, but not one that was ever associated with midwinter. Over time, it shifted and changed, going from a challenge posed as part of a heroic quest, to a challenge proposed by a man who appears at a feast, before finally becoming a challenge proposed by a man appearing at a feast while disguising his appearance with a monstrous outfit. It was at this point that the Gawain poet picked it up and decided, like his King Arthur, that it sounded like a story very suited to Christmastime.

Despite the occasional (fictional) approval of kings, though, the attempts to ban guising were almost as common as the attempts to ban the general Christmas chaos. In London, guising was forbidden from 1405 on, a ban extended to the entirety of England by the time of Henry VIII, who claimed (perhaps not without justification) that some guisers were stealing from the homes they visited. In Scotland, meanwhile, guising was being outlawed in the sixteenth century, when the little town of Elgin forbade the practice. But just as the Kalends bans had little effect, so the guising bans didn't work particularly well either.* The practice survived, and, from the early modern period and into the eighteenth and nineteenth centuries, we have an extraordinary proliferation of sources describing masked, guising creatures at Christmas, many of which have survived to the present day.

---

\* Even with Elgin forbidding guising in the sixteenth-century ban, in the 1600s six men were fined for guising in a churchyard, and the daughter of one Alexander Smith was accused of guising while dressed as a man.

One account, from Shetland in the nineteenth century, describes the custom perfectly – not just the disguises, the house entering, and the begging, but the terror that the costumes and behaviours of the participants inspired. A woman staying on a farm over Christmas in the late 1800s recorded how she:

> saw the kitchen full of beings, whose appearance, being so unearthly, shook the gravity of my muscles, and forced the cold sweat to ooze out of every pore in my body. There they stood like so many statues, one of whom was far above the rest, and of gigantic dimensions. Eyes, mouths, or nose they had none; nor the least trace of a countenance. They kept up an incessant grunt, grunt, grunt ... Their outer garments were white as snow ... They were all *veiled*, and their head dresses or caps were about eighteen inches in height, and made of straw twisted and plaited. The spirits, for such they appeared to be, had long staves, with which they kept rapping the floor.[7]

The creatures 'commenced hobbling and dancing' and then produced a bag, which the householder filled with mutton and oatcakes before they went on their way. If the 'beings' had performed a play instead of a dance, they would have fitted right in at a Marshfield Christmas. We have photos of these creatures from the early twentieth century – strange, haunting black-and-white images of people wearing enormous straw capes and skirts, with straw hats pulled down over their eyes. Often the hats have antler-like extensions made of twisted straw, bizarre protuberances that, when combined with the way the straw capes disrupt the silhouette, give them the shape of something not human at all. They were called skeklars, and were found in the Faroe Islands and Orkney as well as Shetland, until the custom died out in the 1970s. Similar straw costumes are still used today to create the disguises of the Buttnmandln in Bavaria, but these performers also wear horrifying animal masks, which peek through the straw. From a distance, in the twilight, they look utterly monstrous. Animals hides were also used frequently by Christmas guisers – and still are. In Austria and Germany there are plenty of traditional Christmas costumes that look like demonic goats, draped in the skins of animals and covered in furs. Often, the performers also wear goat horns or carve their own from wood, frequently making them abnormally large, two or three feet high. They hide their faces behind hideous and contorted masks, dripping with blood, with elongated tongues and pointed teeth. In Iceland, the performers dress as Grýla, an ogress with fifteen tails, covered in animal skins. In the Nordic countries there is 'Julebukking', which translates as 'Yule Goating'. As suggested by the name, performers dressed up as goats – although from at least the twentieth century on any and all disguises were acceptable, goats or not. In all cases, these monsters are recorded as going door to door at Christmas, knocking and demanding food and drink.

Some of the people going door to door weren't claiming to be demons themselves, but were – supposedly

– preventing the monsters from coming in the first place. In Austria, southern Germany and Switzerland there were the 'Knocking Nights', which were normally defined as the three Thursdays in the run-up to Christmas (although, as with all Christmas traditions they can slide easily from the beginning of December through to Twelfth Night without much trouble). In a sixteenth-century poem, a German scholar described these days:

Three weeks before the day whereon was born the Lord
    of Grace [that is – three weeks before Christmas],
And on the Thursdays boys and girls do run in every place,
And bounce and beat at every door, with blows and lusty
    smacks,
And cry, the Advent of the Lord not born as yet perhaps.
And wishing to the neighbours all, that in the house dwell,
A happy year, and every thing to spring and prosper well:
Here have they pears, and plums and pence, each man
    gives willingly,
For these three nights are always thought, unfortunate
    to be;
Wherein they are afraid of sprites and cankered witches'
    spite,
And dreadful devils black and grim, that then have
    chiefest might.[8]

Here the children are not disguised – instead their blessing works to keep the monsters at bay. But then, in the eighteenth and nineteenth centuries, the tradition shifted again, and the knocking children became

59

the sprites themselves, hiding when they knocked or even carrying poles to tap at windows so it seemed like ghosts were responsible (the poles had the added bonus that the householders could attach treats to them, so the entire thing could be accomplished without the 'ghosts' ever revealing themselves). In the 1800s – especially in Styria and Austria – the knockers became the Glöcklern. Normally grown men, rather than children, these house visitors wore giant paper lanterns on their shoulders – often up to nine feet tall – decorated with cut-outs and bells. The Glöcklern still appear in Austria today, and they are terrifying figures – glowing, towering, battering on doors, demanding to be let in. Even where traditions had shifted to become people doing good by going door to door, bringing luck rather than frights, it seems that the temptation to become monstrous was too much to resist.

This play of monstrousness could become real violence and disruption very quickly. Drunk and disorderly behaviour was common (it was Christmas, after all), as were fines. Very often, in fact, our earliest reference to Christmas guising in a town comes from criminal records: in Uttoxeter, for example, the first account of guisers comes from the court report stating that on 23 December three brothers had 'been out guising and had drink given to them',[9] causing them to assault the police. In 1910, the Uttoxeter guisers were causing problems again – as described in the delightfully titled court report 'Guiser who was a Nuisance', Charles Plant was sent to prison for a month for being drunk and disorderly while guising (this time on 31 December).

Perhaps we might expect the combination of drink and disguises to lead to a certain amount of criminal behaviour, but there is more to it than that, for violence and disorder was and often still is a fundamental part of the tradition. In the little Austrian town of Matrei, the Christmas monsters are called Klaubaufs. Nightmare creatures draped in shaggy pelts and wearing grinning, grotesque wooden masks, they travel from house to house and try to drag the occupants out into the snow. Traditionally, the family inside attempt to protect themselves by hiding behind the kitchen table, which the Klaubaufs try to drag away as well, displaying it outside the house if they are successful. Fights also break out in the street, where the monsters attack passers-by, hurling them to the ground. Such is the violence associated with the Klaubaufs that the night they come through the town requires additional prep for the local A&E, and Matrei makes a point of discouraging tourists from attending.

Not all Christmas monsters are violent, but they all tended to stand for disorder and chaos. As with the Lords of Misrule and the topsy-turvy world of Kalends and Christmas, socially licensed rule-breaking was part of the nature of guising – and one that was only helped by the fact that everyone's identities were hidden.[*] Sometimes the monsters engaged in wild, lewd dancing, spilling

---

[*]   This identity hiding was helped by the fact that, in the tradition of Kalends, many Christmas monsters were also cross-dressing, so that witches were often played by men, and women dressed as men.

61

through the home, demanding their treats with threats of violence that – for this one season – were actively encouraged and rewarded.

In modern times, the household-visiting element of all of this tends to have been abandoned, just as it's all but vanished at Marshfield. Some of this may be down to the loosening of communities – if you know everyone in your little village, you'll likely be happier letting them into your home, even if they are dressed as monsters. Admitting complete strangers would be something else entirely – something genuinely dangerous. Plenty of guisers now go from pub to pub, or, alternatively, participate in parades or runs, which often still retain some hangovers from the old house-visiting tradition. The Klaubaufs, for example, now run through the streets of Matrei as well as knocking on doors, and for those who are unwilling to let the monsters into their home a kitchen table is set up in the centre of the town, for which anyone can wrestle the Klaubaufs. Guising may once have meant allowing chaos and disorder into your private space, but in this bizarre table standing in the snow the practice has been flipped on its head, and the domestic has been pulled outside to meet the demons. To my relief, there's none of that in Marshfield, and now that the ritual parade around the town has been completed, I'm able to curl up in an overstuffed armchair in the corner of the pub, a mug of mulled wine in my hand, without fear of being dragged back out into the cold.

But while the Marshfield paper creatures don't have any particular personalities or stories attached to them, plenty of other Christmas demons developed their own myths and lore, combining with other non-Christmas stories, pulling in witches, demons, ghosts and were-wolves until they loomed frighteningly over the Christmas celebrations. We also can't see whether or not the earliest antlered guisers were intended to be scary (barring that single, suggestive remark from Chrysologos). But whether or not the guisers started out as terrible monsters, they rapidly became so. And whether or not the midwinter season was one of terror in pre-Christian Europe, having hordes of demons lumbering through town over the festive period made it so for everyone who came later. Part and parcel of the tradition of Christmas guising is a whole complex of beliefs that hold that Christmas is a time of genuine darkness, of real monsters and horrors that stalk the midwinter nights. One of the most horrible iterations of these Christmas guises comes, oddly enough, in the form of a horse, and, despite being related to one of the very earliest Christmas monsters, it tends to appear fairly late in the Christmas season – I met it on 20 January, when I went to Wales for a wassail.

# THREE

# Horse Skulls and Hoodenings

*The Chepstow Wassail*
*20 January*

Chepstow castle stands on the craggy limestone cliffs of the Welsh banks of the River Wye, a stronghold built by William the Conqueror to protect the crossing from England into Wales, the little town of Chepstow growing up around it as the centuries passed. One of the oldest castles in Britain, it saw numerous conflicts (and some high-profile imprisonments), but from the seventeenth century on its strategic importance began to decline, and it was all but abandoned, its enormous, sprawling bulk gradually falling into ruins. Today, the only thing its fortifications protect are the handful of tourists wandering inside and, at the foot of its mound under its cracked and bulging grey stone walls, a little orchard, shielded from the wind.

## The Dead of Winter

It's 20 January, which might seem a way out of the Christmas season. But, like plenty of rural places across Europe, some areas of Wales still hold certain celebrations on dates as they would have been in the Julian Calendar, before it was replaced by the Gregorian in the eighteenth century. And according to the Julian Calendar, today is actually 9 January, and therefore the first Saturday after Twelfth Night.* It's damp and bitter – as cold as this winter has been so far – but there's still a crowd standing with me among the bare branches of the orchard. We're here for a wassail – a ceremony to wish good health to the apple trees. And we have help. As we parade through the trees yelling 'wassail' (a word that comes from the Old English for 'be healthy'), as we hang toast on their branches to attract the birds who will fertilise the orchard, as we drink cider and pour a little at the foot of the trees so they can partake as well, we are accompanied by a host of morris dancers, and a parade of grinning monsters.

Shining white in the fading late afternoon light and standing a foot above the crowd, these monsters take the form of horses. Their heads are horse skulls – some plaster casts, some real, and some old enough that the teeth are loose, the bone yellowing. Jammed into their eye sockets are baubles and buttons, glinting in the

---

*     These 'old' dates are also still observed by the Orthodox Church, which still bases its liturgy on the old Julian Calendar, so that plenty of Eastern Orthodox Christians celebrate Christmas on 7 January.

half-light. One has whirling LEDs for eyes, which, as the afternoon slips into evening and the darkness grows heavier, throw ever deeper shadows into the hollows of the skull. The heads are decorated in other ways as well – some have designs carved onto the bone, others wear veils or crowns of mistletoe, or have ribbons streaming down their backs. One has a bauble swinging from its jaw, the thread wedged in between its teeth.

The skulls are held on poles by a person who hides under a sheet. The shape under the sheet is almost as uncanny as the skull itself, sometimes bowed forward so it looks like a quadruped without its front legs, sometimes standing nearly upright so it looks almost human but with a wide and grossly elongated neck and no arms, profoundly and indefinably wrong either way. In most cases the performers are wearing normal jeans and trainers, visible under the white sheet that only reaches their knees, the mundanity blending into the surreal monster and making it more surreal still.

And the horse skulls aren't motionless. Most are rigged so the performer can use a stick to open and shut the jaw, bone clacking against bone as the animal swings round, lunging at people, the shape beneath the sheet writhing and distorting as they move. They're mischievous: stealing hats, scaring people by snapping their jaws at them, chasing after little children, all while the horse's skull grins its delirious, rictus smile. The children are nervously delighted by the horror. Before the wassail, one little girl sitting on her father's shoulders repeats to herself, 'The horses can't hurt me,' and then, after screaming when they appear, insists that she be allowed to go over and pet one. When a horse I'm standing behind suddenly swings round to face me, snapping at me, grinning, lunging forward, I could do with a bit of her courage.

These monsters are called Mari Lwyds, a name that might mean 'grey mare' – the 'mari' likely taken from the English 'mare' and the 'lwyd' coming from the Welsh for grey, a combination that seems perfect in a Welsh town where we can see England on just the other side of the river. Each Mari is part of a different morris group that has come for the wassail, and each has a leader, holding the horse by its reigns and guiding the performer over the treacherously muddy ground of the orchard.

The Maris, we're told, are here to help scare away any evil spirits that might harm the apple trees. We're led in a wordless, aggressive howl, and the Maris buck and whiny, their ghastly hunchbacked shapes braying among the bare branches. The shouts drift on the freezing air, echoing across the castle walls and the river. It's difficult to believe there might be something here that is even more terrifying than the horses, something which requires the six Maris with us and our shouting to drive it away.

The Mari Lwyds are not only to be found in Chepstow. They appear across South Wales, emerging at Christmastime and lingering until Old Twelfth Night, ghastly and unsettling monsters loping through towns and orchards. But what might be most surprising about the Mari Lwyds is that something very like them appears not just in the rest of the UK, but across Europe – an uncanny, sheet-clad being, holding an animal's head on a pole and running across the continent over the Christmas season, snapping its jaws at the unwary. But before we can look at these monsters, we need to clear up an issue with wassailing. Because there's something very confusing going on in the orchards of Chepstow.

Tell someone in the UK that you're going to a wassail and those who recognise the term will tend to associate it with apples. They might even have gone to one of the frequently sold-out events at local orchards or cider breweries and have spent an afternoon or evening parading around trees carrying flaming torches, hanging toast on the branches, or sipping from a communal wassail bowl – a large, polished wooden bowl of cider (or, in these more germ-conscious times, sipping from a disposable paper cup that's been filled from the bowl).* There are hundreds of wassails like this scattered across the UK, and they're growing ever more popular – in 2024 the *Daily Telegraph* even suggested that wassailing was 'what our broken society needs'.† They are, to a one, delightful ways to spend time – but this complete

---

\*  If you're wondering whether people milk the pun of 'toasting' the trees by hanging toast on them, and 'toasting' the trees with a drink, the answer is yes. If you go to a wassail, be prepared to be sick of this wordplay within the first half-hour.

†  I'm as pro wassailing as the next person, but I am baffled by a newspaper that thinks wassails are what will mend our society rather than a re-instatement of the social safety net, and perhaps a touch less racism, misogyny and transphobia.

domination of orchard wassailing means we're losing a different definition of the word. The existence of this second type of wassailing becomes much more obvious when, at Chepstow, after the Maris have whinnied in the trees and we've drunk our cider, we break into a 'wassail song', chanted uncertainly by the crowd to the trilling of a piper, whose music is snatched away with every gust of wind. The words are just about audible, but they're also printed on the programme that's been given out for the event:

Oh master and missus, are you all within?
Pray open the door and let us come in,
Oh master and missus who sit by the fire,
Pray think of the travellers who walk through the mire.

Oh where is the maid with the silver hairpin,
To open the door and let us come in?
Oh master and missus, it is our desire,
A good load of cheese and a toast by the fire.

After a few more verses, the song concludes that 'This is the night we go singing Wassail'. None of it concerns apples (which don't get a single mention) – but it should sound very familiar: it's about guising. We're standing among the apple trees, in front of a ruined castle, with no residences in sight (unless you want to stretch the definition and count the tourist information office) and we're singing a song about wassailing by going house to house demanding food and drink.

The word 'wassail' first appeared in the eighth century in the poem *Beowulf*, and seems to have been a toast (at the very least, it was a shout that should echo through courts and begin the revels of warriors). By the fourteenth century, we have mentions of communal drinking bowls that could be passed person to person with cries of 'wassail' and 'drinkhail' and an exchange of kisses. And while cheery toasting at mass get-togethers sounds very Christmassy, it was only in the sixteenth century that wassail bowls are firmly placed in the Christmas season, appearing at a Twelfth Night party in Henley in England. Their Christmas popularity grew, though, so that eventually even Henry VIII had his own wassail bowl. By the seventeenth century, groups of women were taking the bowl door to door and offering a drink in exchange for food or money. Soon, monsters were tagging along on the visits, as the wassailing tradition melded with Christmas door-to-door guising, and the bowl, more often than not, was left at home. By the nineteenth century wassailing could be just another word for Christmas guising – no apples or bowls necessary. This was the wassailing to which the Mari Lwyd was originally attached.

But from the late sixteenth century on in Southern England, wassailing had moved in another direction. Instead of taking the bowl house to house, wassailing groups would take it into the orchards or fields over Christmas and the New Year to bid good health to trees and crops. Other bits were added to this orchard wassailing – offering bread to the trees (or hanging it from the branches to attract birds), pouring out a little of the wassail bowl at the roots, and separate wassail songs, which, unlike the Chepstow wassail song, really were about orchards. By the eighteenth century, people were lighting fires among the trees as well, bringing a little light and warmth to the orchard during the darkest, coldest time of the year. When the idea of driving out evil spirits came to be attached to all of this is unclear – there was certainly a lot of shouting going on in some eighteenth-century wassailing, but the recorded rituals tended to involve toasting to the success of the crops in the next year: an attempt to bring good luck, rather than drive out the bad. It seems like a fairly modern idea that the wassail should be used to repel evil, but it's part of the ceremonies now, a letting off of steam where you can yell and bellow or bash pans and cymbals. But with orchard wassails typically taking place in England, the Mari Lwyd would traditionally have participated in a door-to-door visiting wassail, and would never – normally – have set foot in an orchard.

The celebration at Cheptsow is a joyous combining of both types of wassail – held in an orchard but attended by guising monsters who participate in the rituals, and finished with a song about going door to door begging for food and drink. And it's coming to other places in Wales as well – the Blackthorn Wassail held by Newton Court Cider is another orchard wassailing, with plenty of Mari Lwyds in attendance, monsters that have, late in life, turned to driving out evil rather than just causing it.

On Old New Year (13 January)* I'm in the village of
Maestag in the Llynfi Valley, somewhere between Cardiff
and Swansea, in the Corner House Inn.† About three-
quarters of the building has been turned into a modern
gastro pub, but a little corner tucked away under the low,
beamed ceiling is still a standing bar. On the night of the
wassail, it's completely packed – fifty of us crammed
into the tiny area and doing our best not to bother the
diners in the rest of the building. There's a roaring fire,
good drink and good company, all in glorious contrast
to the night outside, which is hard and brilliant, lit by
a whisker of an orange moon. But something is coming up the valley, through the darkness, to knock on the
door.

I have to admit, I don't hear the knock over the sound
of merry-making in the pub, but we all feel the cold blast
of air as the door is opened by the landlord, and turn to
look. There are two figures standing on the threshold –
a man dressed in a top hat and black suit, and the Mari,

---

\* As with Old Twelfth Night, this is the day that would have been the
New Year before the Gregorian calendar came into effect.

† Until a few years ago this event used to take place at the Old House
pub, just over the road. The Old House even had a Mari Lwyd on its
sign, but in recent years has been given over to high-end weddings
and is less inclined to welcome skeletal horses (my strong feeling is
that a skeletal horse would perk up any wedding – and that my hus-
band, who married me during the Mari Lwyd season, on 7 January
2017, is lucky the idea didn't occur to me then). The bonus of this
new location is that the Corner House is supposedly haunted by
the ghost of a poet who is buried across the way in Maestag's little
churchyard.

which he leads on a bridle. The Mari's skull is piled high with decorations – ribbons and rosettes, little plastic sprigs of holly, black streamers that fall down its back like a mane, and two green baubles glinting its eyes. From its mouth dangles a bell. Unlike the performers at Chepstow, who come from across the region to perform, these two are well known in the village – or at least, the horse's head and its leader are (the man beneath the sheet remains a mystery). The leader is Gwyn Evans, who was given his role and the skull by his father, who had fulfilled a similar role in the village for decades, a longevity that makes it feel imbedded in the community, bound to the village and inherent to it.

Indeed, this tradition has deep roots in Wales. The appearance of the Mari as a guising monster, knocking on houses to beg for food, drink and money is first attested in the eighteenth century in Wales, where:

> they would carry a man ... dressed in presentable clothes, and adorned with all manner of multi-coloured ribbons, and an old horse's skull on his head, being carried along the roads by three or four strong and senseless men, calling at every door in the village for charity and for everyone's goodwill.[1]

According to tradition, when the Mari party calls at the door, you might just be able to avoid letting them in – as long as you're a good enough poet and can hold a tune. Right now, standing on the threshold of the Maestag

Corner House, Gwyn Evans breaks into song – a beautifully rich baritone that resounds through the little pub. The words are in Welsh, but a handy translation has been provided in a little printed leaflet I've been given:

> Well here we come,
> Harmless friends,
> To ask permission
> To sing.

This is the beginning of a *'pwnco'*, a rhyming call-and-response game that was once carried out between the Mari party and the residents of whatever house they'd chosen to approach. If the householders wanted the ghostly horse and its retinue gone, they'd have to outwit them in the game. We do have some surviving records of responses to the Mari Lwyd. Normally, they attack the rhyming and singing abilities of the Mari party ('The dogs and the cats are retreating into the holes on hearing such voices' or perhaps 'The kettle and the frying pan are bouncing on the hearthstone on hearing such low quality rhyme'[2]). But these formulaic survivals are not a perfect preservation of the practice. In many cases we hear of the rhyming being spontaneous – lyrical insults conjured on the spot. There is an account of one such battle in 1850, when a householder decided that the Mari party were not welcome in his house, given that they'd caused chaos there the year before, and used his skilful versifying to win the *pwnco* and drive the monster away.* But by 1909, people were already mourning that the 'ready rhymesters' and 'genuine wits'[3] who had previously given the *pwnco* such creativity and excitement, were gone. The formulaic call and response were what remained.

There is no response to the Mari's *pwnco* at the Corner House in Maestag, formulaic or otherwise. After the singing stops the leader and his Mari enter, unhindered and unchallenged. They circle the pub, through the dining area with its nice carpets and reserved tables (and the bright pink balloons and sashes of a twenty-first-birthday dinner party, whose attendees are surprised and not entirely pleased about the ghostly horse intruding on the celebration). It seems much smaller than the older Mari wassails, when a gang would have accompanied the horse for the call-and-response games at the door. Even by the late nineteenth century the decline of the Mari Lwyd had started, and sources began recording it as a tradition that 'used to be widespread'. By 1929, people were already talking about reviving the tradition, rather than continuing it.† It survived, barely, over the decades, but it's been growing vastly in popularity in the last few

---

* Heartbreakingly, none of the rhymes themselves were actually recorded.

† Reviving a tradition that called for a real horse's skull feels more unpleasant than reviving – say – a mummers play. In one case, the would-be Mari Lwyd party 'knew a horse had been buried in Kimberly Moor, years and years before, so we went and dug it up, and sure enough the head was good as new, the real thing.'

years, which have seen the appearance of the Chepstow wassail and its herd of Maris, and horse skulls popping up all across Wales at Christmastime. Perhaps it's only a matter of time until the Mari Lwyd of Maestag is restored to its full glory.

The Mari Lwyd may seem like a uniquely peculiar tradition, but in fact, it is a local variation of a ritual that can be found scattered right across the UK. One 1807 account from Ramsgate in Kent describes how, at Christmas:

> a party of young people procure the head of a dead horse, which is affixed to a pole about ten feet in length, and a string is affixed to the lower jaw: a horse-cloth is also attached to the whole under which a member of the part gets, and by frequently pulling the string, keeps up a loud snapping noise and is accompanied by the rest of the party, grotesquely habited, with hand bells, they thus process from house to house, ringing their bells and singing carols and songs; they are commonly gratified with beer and cake, or perhaps money.[4]

This might be an account of any Mari Lwyd (barring the astonishing length of the pole), but here in England it was called a Hoodening – a term likely referring to the fact that the performer was hooded by the sheet. And like the Mari Lwyd, the hoodening tradition continues to be enacted, normally in Kent, Yorkshire and Derbyshire

– although most, now, use wooden horse heads rather than skulls.[*]

By all rights, the wooden version should be a lot less terrifying, but there is something utterly, intentionally unsettling about every one of the hoodening heads. The hooden horse from Walmer Court, dating to the 1850s and held in the Deal Museum, is a perfect example. Decorated with red and white rosettes, and with a trio of bells perched on its head, it's made from two flat rectangles of wood painted a dark muddy brown. The two rectangles are hinged at one end to made a snapping jaw, with little carved wooden teeth at the front. With its long, thin snout and gaping mouth it looks more like a strange alligator than a horse. A leather bridle snakes its way over the head, and on the top are two painted eyes – white circles with a black dot in the middle, wild and staring. Two leather ears, nailed in place, stick out at the top of the head, the crumbling orange cloth that the performed hid under hanging from the back. A string to open and shut the mouth comes through a hole on the top of the head, the wood around it worn down from the repeated pulling. We even have a photo of the monster in action, taken in 1907. In it, the performer is standing upright under the sheet, his shape making the creature

---

[*]  The use of the horse's skull for these non-Welsh horses isn't just attested in the account from Ramsgate. There was also a horse skull, with baubles crammed into its eyes, found in a lake in Hooten Pagnell Hall in Yorkshire. Supposedly, it had been tossed there in frustration by a party of hoodeners in the 1880s, disappointed by the 'meagre returns' of their door-to-door visits.

look like a weird, bipedal hunchback, the manic smile of its open mouth just as bad as any grinning skull. Three men are standing with the animal. One holding the reins, the two others carrying an accordion and a tambourine. The rhyming *pwnco* was limited to Wales, but songs still accompanied the hooden horses of Kent, normally popular music-hall tunes, performed at the households the hoodeners visited. In other cases they gave plays – often variants of mummers plays, shifted to accommodate the fact that they needed a horse to be a central character. Usually, they were about the horse dying, just as Little Man John does in the Marshfield play, to be revived by the doctor jamming a comically huge pill into its mouth.

None of the other hooden horses I've seen look any more pleasant – the snapping jaws, the wide, frenzied eyes, the strange sheeted shapes, are there in every version. Not all horses were intended to stand upright. In some cases the performer bent forwards, leaning on two sticks which worked as the animal's front legs, so the horse appeared to be on all fours. There is something amusing in hooden horses – they all look like they're smiling, even laughing, albeit that they're huge, demented smiles, and the wide eyes make them look almost mad. One book on hooden horses is called 'Discordant Comicals', which is a good way of describing them – fear and humour combining. I found that mix in the Mari Lwyds as well, skulls that stole hats and pranked. And of course, the terror is part of the joke too – everyone who jumps when a Mari Lwyd snaps at them laughs immediately afterwards, amused at their own fear.

But it wasn't just in the UK where these types of snapping sheet-and-stick monsters emerged in the eighteenth century to terrorise the countryside every Christmas. The English hoodeners and the Welsh Maris would only have needed to add a pair of antlers to their heads to fit right in across Europe.

In the Vienna Folklore Museum is a yellowing wooden goat head on a pole. It has flapping black ears, short, curved horns, wide black eyes and an enormous, gaping, snapping mouth, lined with sharp little rows of carved wooden teeth. The jaw is rigged so that it snaps closed when the performer, holding the pole and hidden beneath a sheet, pulls on a thin piece of string dangling from the back of the monster's head. This creature is called a Habergeiß, a name almost certainly related to goats (*'geiß'* is the Austrian for goat) and it can be found prowling the streets and snapping at the unwary in Bavarian towns over Epiphany.[*] Over in Poland there's the Turon, another horned, shaggy monster head with a clacking jaw that's held on a pole by a performer under a sheet. The Turon is led on a rope house to house, where its escort sings carols and the Turon jumps and claps his jaw, chasing the householders. In Romania there are the Corlata, monsters who appear at

---

[*] The pole on which the Habergeiß's head is held can be many feet tall, so it towers over the spectators – perhaps suggesting that while the ten-foot pole attributed to the Ramsgate Hoodeners might be an exaggeration, it wasn't unprecedented.

the end of the year led by groups visiting houses, and are made from (you'll never guess) a horned, wooden head – a stag's, this time – with a clacking jaw, held on a pole by a performer who hides under a sheet (although the sheet that covers the Corlata can often be extremely brightly patterned – one photograph from 2010 shows it covered in brilliant flowers). In North-East Germany there's the Klapperbock (the snapping buck), in the Italian Tyrol there are the Schanppvieh – snapbeasts (although these normally appeared at Carnival rather than Christmas). In Switzerland there's the Schnabelgeiß, the 'beak goat', which looks like all the other goat monsters except that the snout narrows to a point, to take the form of a beak. In Finland and Sweden there are the Nuuttipukki, more stags who bother householders, this time on St Knut's Day, on 13 January (hence their name). And we've already come across the Finnish Julebukk – the Yule goat – another goat monster portrayed by a performer hiding under a sheet, this time made of animal hides. In some parts of Lithuania and Silesia, meanwhile, there was the Schimmelreiter – the grey rider – which came with a new innovation. As in Britain, this monster was a horse, with a snapping head that was often a horse's skull held on a pole, but this one was played by multiple people and could be ridden.* It

---

\*  It was also the subject of *The Rider on the White Horse*, the haunting 1888 novel by Theodor Storm, where a surveyor in Northern Frisia finds tales of a ghostly, skeleton horse and its mournful rider. Despite not mentioning Christmas at any point in the narrative, it's a tremendous read on a winter evening.

starts to feel like you can't go to Europe over the Christmas period without being snapped at by an animal head on a pole, held by a performer lurking under a cloth.

It seems likely that this vast horde of horned, snapping monsters running about over Christmas were related to the stags, bulls and goats of Kalends celebrations of Late Antiquity. Although many of the names for the monsters are first attested in the nineteenth century, as we have seen the complaints about people dressing as horned beasts over Christmas runs right through from Late Antiquity to the early modern period. Remember those comments from the thirteenth century about people dressing as 'wild animals' at Kalends? Throughout the fifteenth century in Austria and Germany there are references to house-to-house visits by a 'billy goat' during the Christmas season.

But it's not just that the modern snapping-head monsters are related to the Christmas guising because both traditions involve horned animals going house to house over midwinter: it's possible that the outfit itself – the head on the pole, the sheet covering the performer – is at least close to the disguise people wore in the fourth century BC. The descriptions in the early accounts are lost, but we do know that some guising involved animal 'heads' (rather than masks) and animal skins, which might have been used like the sheets to conceal the person carrying a head. In fact, we may even have a fourteenth-century image of the costumes, from the marginalia of a Flemish manuscript. It shows a man who has dressed himself as a stag by (say it with me) holding a stag's head on a pole while hiding under an animal skin that comes down to his knees, his shoed and stockinged feet visible beneath. The mouth of the stag lolls open in a flat, giddy smile, and the face of the performer is visible under it, peeping through the animal skin in the place where the animal's neck should be. Whenever a Mari lost its leader at Chepstow I saw the same thing: faces peeking out, just under the neck of the monster. For a seven-hundred-year-old image, it looks astonishingly familiar.

There is a gap of about three to four hundred years where the Christmas horned monsters aren't attested in the sources, where the complaining churchmen found other things to moan about, and the folklorists had yet to appear. It is, technically, possible that the tradition of parading snapping, horned animal heads on poles at Christmastime died out across Europe in the fifteenth century, and then re-appeared during the eighteenth in a completely unconnected form that happened to look extremely similar. But it feels like the simplest explanation is that the traditions were related, that the Christmas horned animal costumes of the eighteenth, nineteenth and twentieth centuries were an extension of the Christmas stag guises from Late Antiquity and the Middle Ages.

But this doesn't mean that stag playing was always as widespread as the modern snapping monsters are. In fact, one place in particular seems to have been a late adopter of the practice – Britain. There are no complaints about people running around as monsters or animals over the Christmas period in Britain in early antiquity. In fact, in the seventh century, Theodore, the Archbishop of Canterbury, issued a penitential which read exactly like every other penitential of the period – except that it notably left out any comments about people dressing as animals at Kalends. That was until it was copied by a cleric working in Germany or France, who immediately added them in. It strongly implies that at least in the seventh century these sorts of animal guises were not being used in Britain as they were on the continent.

This might also explain why Britain is so resolutely attached to equine snap-beasts, rather than ones with antlers. In fact, it has been suggested that the snapping monsters didn't make it to England until the late medieval period, which coincided with a growing popularity for a mock-horse costume, that consisted of a model horse sitting on the performers hips, with fake legs hanging down the side, so it looked as though the performer was actually riding the animal. These seem to have been used in dances (and perhaps even mock tournaments), until, by the early modern period, they'd snuck into Christmas celebrations. It is possible that these horse costumes combined with the continental snapping animal heads on poles – which were, after all, much easier to tote round and make, not to mention much more horrifying – to become the Mari Lwyd and hooden horses of the modern day, to gallop across the country over the Christmas season frightening everyone they met.

Standing in the pub at Maestag, waiting for the Mari Lwyd to make its way through the crowd, the woman next to me tells me how her grandmother hated the Mari, that it was led by an unruly gang of boys who would force entry into her parents' house and refuse to leave until they'd eaten and drunk everything in sight. 'The Mari Lwyd who came to tea,' laughs someone standing next to me. The current Mari, edging its way through the bar, is collecting for charities and, in a joltingly surreal conversation that you don't expect to have with a skeleton horse, pleasantly asks me if I've come far as he poses for a photo. I wouldn't want a raucous gang to turn up at my door demanding entrance, food, and drink, with or without a horse-skull monster accompanying them, but something does feel lost in the domestication of it all. Barring the occasional hat stealing, so much of the menace has been drained from the tradition. Mari Lwyds even turn up in churches now, as part of January services, dancing down the aisle with the full approval of the clergy – and in their new, more benevolent form, I'm not convinced that even the churchmen of Late Antiquity would have objected (much). I find myself mildly disappointed. But, as the Mari begins to walk away, the performer struggles briefly with the pole, which twists in his hands, the skull turning to face me, lolling at an angle, the firelight catching the baubles in its eyes and making them shine at me through the smoky air of the pub. Seeing the nightmarish, grinning face stuck with bits of tinsel, there's just a glint of the old terror.

*The Dead of Winter*

The Welsh Mari Lwyd may now be a largely peace-able affair, but elsewhere in Europe we can meet another descendent of the horned snapping beasts – one which hasn't yet been tamed, and who prowls through Austria and Germany every winter, on the night of 5 December.

# FOUR

# Punishing the Wicked

### The Salzburg Krampus Run
### 5 December

For the entirety of December Salzburg Old Town is a glorious sparkle of Christmas markets, gluhwein and greenery-twined fairy lights, set against the baroque splendour of Salzburg Cathedral. A tangle of tiny streets that open onto churches and little market squares and full of buildings that date back to the Middle Ages, it's dominated by the towering Hoehensalzburg Fortress, and, beyond that, the Untersberg Mountain, which represents the beginning of the Alps. It looks like a fantasy realm even in the summer, and when I arrive in early December the effect is only enhanced by the thick blanket of snow that covers the city.* As the flakes drift through the

---

\*  It's the tail end of a serious cold snap in Europe, which saw incredible quantities of snow fall, especially in Austria and Southern Germany. Salzburg, when I visit, is full of travellers trying to get to Munich who have reached Austria and can go no further.

sweet, spiced air, reflected in the glittering baubles that spill from market stalls and shop windows, it's hard to imagine something more traditionally Christmassy.

But as the sun sets on 5 December, there's a strange, tense excitement hanging over the Old Town. The streets are packed (especially for a bitterly cold Tuesday night) and filled with nervous laughter. As I walk through the Old Market Square a group of teenagers runs past, giggling, jittery, grabbing each other from behind to give each other a scare. They're going the same way I am and I follow them down onto the main thoroughfare of the old town – Getreidegasse. There are fairy lights strung between the buildings and filling shop windows, and the route is lined with people on each side, sometimes two rows deep. While there are plenty of adults and teenagers, there's a large number of families with children in attendance as well. I find my own space among them and wait.

And then, slowly, I realise I can hear something – a low, jangling discordant music accompanied by screaming laughter, faint at first but growing ever louder, ever closer. I catch a glimpse of curling, gigantic horns silhouetted against the Christmas lights, and then, suddenly, the street is swarming with monsters. With masks depicting terrifying leering grimaces, mouths filled with jagged teeth, huge horns (often over a metre high), and costumes of shaggy pelts, these are the Krampuses. They are enormous – many of the Krampus performers wear platforms on their shoes to give them extra height, and the bulk of the pelts and horns make them even larger, towering over the spectators. They walk with a loping, swinging tread that only renders them more menacing, more animalistic, and serves to shake the giant cowbells that are strapped to their backs – this is the hideous music that accompanies them, so loud you have to yell to be heard. Every Krampus carries a switch.

As the first of the monsters reach us, two of them seize a young boy standing across from me. He tries to duck away, laughing, but the Krampuses each grab one of his arms, looming over him. They raise their switches and bring them down on his legs before releasing him, pushing him back into the crowd. Next to me are a group of girls, who have picked a spot by a narrow ginnel that leads away from the street. A Krampus with a haunting, white face jumps at them and they sprint away down the passage, but the monster follows, chasing them and grabbing at them, swatting them with his switch when he catches them until they return giggling and breathless.

And then a particularly fearsome monster crosses in front of me. He's tall, even for a Krampus, with giant horns that curl like a ram's.* His body is entirely covered with black, shaggy fur and his wooden mask is contorted into a vicious, open-mouthed snarl, showing cracked blackened teeth, each one longer than my little finger. I think he's passed me, but he suddenly turns back,

---

\* I'm using male pronouns here, but there are some female performers (and plenty of tedious men who insist women shouldn't be taking part) – and of course, under pelts and masks it's impossible to guess gender.

lunging at me with outspread arms. I jump away, startled, terrified, laughing. He lunges again, reaching for me with an enormous clawed hand, switch raised, and I realise I'm backed against the wall – there's nowhere for me to run as he swats me with the little bundle of sticks, before loping off, running to the opposite side of the street to do the same thing to someone else.

And it doesn't stop. The procession lasts about half an hour, and never thins. Hundreds of monsters prowl past, and for every one that doesn't notice me there's another who switches me, or grabs me, or jumps close to scare me. Soon I and all the other spectators are breathless with laughter and screaming, with running and dodging only to find ourselves cornered by another monster. Often they double back, creeping up behind you as you're looking down the street at the next host of Krampuses, waiting for you to realise that there's something dark and terrible looming at your back, sticks raised, ready to strike. One mischievously steals my hat, forcing me to run into the horde of monsters to reclaim it. Being among them feels utterly terrifying – their great snarling bulks surrounding me, grabbing me and hitting me, even if only lightly. Other people are physically dragged into the parade by one or more of the demons, pulled and pushed in the fray before being firmly switched and released to run back to relative safety at the side of the street. And while the Krampuses are very happy to target adults, their focus is on the many children who have been brought by their families, jumping at them and snarling, reaching out their clawed hands to toddlers and tweens.* Krampus is, after all, the punisher of misbehaving children. He is the antithesis of Santa, who, rather than giving gifts to the good, spends his Christmastime switching, beating and kidnapping the bad. If you're used to a twinkly eyed Santa beaming kindly at little boys and girls at this time of year, perhaps the only thing more disturbing than having huge monsters attack you is watching them pick off children in the crowd.

Except that Santa is involved in all of this too – the figure who is meant to control the Krampus is Santa's precursor: St Nicholas himself. This relationship is the reason that Krampus Night is on the 5th, with the saint's day following it on the 6th. I spot St Nicholas in the parade tonight as well, a single man wearing a red-and-gold bishop's outfit and a white beard, wandering with a faintly ineffectual benevolence as his monsters rampage through the streets. He's supposed to approve of what they're doing – they're his monsters, under his power – but even if he didn't, he doesn't look capable of stopping them. The feeling of barely contained chaos is present in the reality of the parade as well. At certain stages there are people in high-vis jackets ushering the Krampuses along, but the monsters frequently ignore

---

\* There's a long-running discussion about whether or not the Krampus runs are cruel to children. It would certainly be a profoundly horrible thing to do if a child was genuinely scared, but every child I saw was having a wonderful time, and all the screaming was immediately followed by laughter. I'm sure there are children who would find the whole thing upsetting, but I assume their parents wouldn't bring them.

them, or even attack them. Is it really all in play? There are other hints of genuine violence too – about halfway through the parade a young man smoking a cigarette pushes past the crowd and starts walking down the middle of the street, feigning nonchalance. He's not explicitly challenging the Krampuses, but by ignoring them and refusing to respect the parade he might as well be. Three Krampuses lunge at him and start snarling, jostling him, switching him – noticeably harder than they've hit me or anyone nearby. For a brief moment, his indifference vanishes and he looks scared, angry. Someone in a high-vis jacket runs over and pulls him out, but what would have happened if the volunteer hadn't noticed – or if the Krampuses had refused to stop? What if the young man had struck back? The threatened violence is a joke, a play, until suddenly you worry that it might not be. It adds a new layer of terrifying excitement, like riding a roller-coaster when you're scared the track might collapse.

Even the regular spectators aren't entirely safe. Plenty of the Krampuses carry switches made of grass – impossible to hurt anyone with even if they tried. But some carry bunches of birch sticks instead, and while they're only supposed to hit you lightly you have to trust that they're gauging their strength and distance from you correctly, in the darkness, with everyone running, while they're wearing masks that partially obscure their vision. You also have to trust that they want to. Towards the end of the parade a Krampus charges up behind me when I'm standing still and swipes me with his sticks so hard it makes me cry out in genuine pain. When I get back to my hotel room later that night and take off my jeans, I find angry red welts across the backs of my legs, the skin around them already turning purple. It's deep into January before they're completely healed. Perhaps this is a close as I'll get to true guising – not the staid ritual of the modern hoodenings but roiling chaos that strays, at times, close to real danger, all played out in the snow and under the glittering lights of a Salzburg Christmas.

There are plenty of variants of Krampus runs scattered through Europe, especially in the Alpine regions. In some, the performers are separated from the public by metal fencing and the worst the monsters can do is rattle the railings or swipe at the spectators standing too close. Given the mayhem of Salzburg, I can see why some town councils and attendees prefer to be a little safer and a little more removed from the Krampuses (though if I'm entirely honest, it sounds a lot less fun). In other places, the spectacle is more stage managed, with pyrotechnics, fog effects, and a soundtrack of heavy metal rather than clanking cow bells. In some places, modern additions to the Krampus outfits, like glowing LED eyes, are forbidden, in others they're happily embraced. Plenty of Krampus groups do house calls as well as the main run (some, joyously, allow for house visits to be booked online on the Krampus group's website). In other places, the Krampuses take part in a short play with St Nicholas before they rampage through the town.

The large parades are normally made up of multiple small groups of performers, called Passes, from the surrounding areas. But the Passes can act independently as well – on my first night in Salzburg I found a group of ten Krampuses terrorising one of the smaller markets, complete with their own St Nicholas to marshal the monsters. At another Krampus event, dozens of separate Passes were brought up individually onto a stage in front of Salzburg Cathedral and introduced to the crowd. As the groups passed each other coming on and off the stage they engaged in mock fights. These ritualised combats between groups are such an important part of some Krampus performances that they even have a name – *Rempler* (a word that means 'jostling' in German) – and it's perhaps unsurprising that in less-managed events they can lead to injuries.

But as well as being the organisational backbone of the Krampus runs, the Passes show that the Krampus tradition is more fragmented than it might otherwise appear. Even on the tourist website advertising the Salzburg events, clicking through to the pages for the participating Passes will show you that many don't call themselves Krampuses, but use the name 'Perchten'. Looking beyond Salzburg, there are plenty of other terms for the monsters as well – 'Klaubauf' is common, as is 'Kramperl', 'Ganggerl' and 'Toifi'. Sometimes there are superficial differences between the monsters (the Klaubaufs doesn't usually have horns, whereas Krampuses and Perchten do), but the traditions surrounding them are almost identical, and you'd be hard pressed to tell them apart on a dark night. And there are other names associated with dark Santa attendants as well – Belsnickel, Père Fouettard, Knecht Ruprecht. To understand the vast swirl of folklore associated with these monsters, we first need to look at the man who walks with them.

Just before the Krampus run, I came across the St Nicholas pacing around the Old Market Square, occasionally posing for photos. With his bishop's hat and crozier and glittering gold-and-red robes he was firmly the saint, rather than Santa Claus[*] – there was no welcoming jollity and warmth in the tall, thin bishop, and I certainly wouldn't have wanted to sit on his knee or find him coming down my chimney. Even in his own legends, St Nicholas cuts quite a severe, even violent, figure – in one (likely untrue) story, he punched someone he disagreed with at the council of Nicaea.[†] The children at the Krampus run seemed to share my view of the Nicholas – standing a little distance away from the saint is a howling child who's terrified to go anywhere near him, crying

---

[*]    Although Santa Claus's name comes from St Nicholas, by way of the Dutch Sinterklaas, the fat, jolly, reindeer-flying version of Santa would only begin to appear in the nineteenth century.

[†]    Admittedly, that someone was Arius, who was responsible for a controversial popular doctrine that the son of God was produced by the father of God, but even in the face of such heresy, only Santa was inclined to throw hands.

the only tears I see all evening while his mother tries to coax him into going up for a photo.

For a saint who has left such a lasting mark upon our Christmas traditions, we know vanishingly little about the historical St Nicholas. The most we can really say is that he likely lived in the fourth century and may have been bishop of Myra, a Byzantine city in what is now Southern Turkey.* By the ninth century, however, his legend involved three main miracles – in one he saved the lives of three men who had been wrongly sentenced to death, and in another he calmed a storm. The final miracle, though, was to have the biggest influence over his future myth. Supposedly, Nicholas heard of a man who was so impoverished that he was considering selling his three young daughters into prostitution. Deciding to save the girls but unwilling to reveal his generosity, Nicholas tossed three bags of gold into their house over the course of three nights, each bag representing a dowry for one of the girls. This story of secret, night-time gift-giving captured the popular imagination and was frequently represented in art across Europe, with the saint normally depicted in a hood so as to further mask his identity. In remembrance of Nicholas's charity presents were often given to family, friends and the poor on 6 December – a date that had been set as Nicholas's saint's day back in the fourth century – and had quickly become associated with the opening of the Christmas season. By the

---

\* Though even these simple facts come to us from sources long after his death.

sixteenth century, giving gifts on Nicholas's Day was so common that Martin Luther – in an effort to diminish the importance of saint's days – was insisting that everyone should only be giving presents on Christmas Day. Not that it worked – giving gifts on the night of the 5th is still common, especially in Germany, the Netherlands and Eastern Europe, with the saint leaving treats tucked into children's shoes to be found on the morning of the 6th.

But there were other, stranger legends in which St Nicholas helped children. By the time the Norman poet Wace wrote his life of Nicholas in the eleventh century, the saint was saving a baby who'd been accidentally left in a pot of water hanging over a fire* and driving a demon out of a misbehaving child. Wace also recorded a tale of three young boys who were travelling to start their new life as clerks at a monastery and took lodgings at an inn on the way, only to be robbed, murdered and dismembered by the innkeeper and his wife. They were saved by a passing St Nicholas who forced the innkeeper to confess his guilt and miraculously resurrected the clerks from the heap of flesh and limbs. This story was almost as popular as the tale of Nicholas's gift-giving and was frequently represented in medieval art – three little figures, often

---

\* You might think that's quite a hard thing to do accidentally, but the mother was trying to give the infant a warm bath by putting it in a pot over open flames, suddenly remembered that St Nicholas was giving a sermon at the cathedral, and in her excitement forgot the baby and rushed off to attend – surely a situation familiar to us all.

with their new tonsures, arising from the dead while the murderer and his wife look on with guilty fear. Both the gift-giving and the child-resurrecting were also the subject of some of the very earliest church plays about Nicholas, performed every 6 December.

Perhaps it was the fact that Nicholas helped clerks newly out of school, and a disobedient, demon-possessed boy, that lent a stricter, disciplinary element to Nicholas's interventions with children. By the 1600s, a school in Innsbruck had a man dressed as St Nicholas who visited each of the students in turn, quizzing them on their studies. Only those who passed his tests would be rewarded with gifts. Which left a question hanging over everything – if good children received presents, what did the bad children get?

In an impossibly boringly named book *German Single Leaf Woodcuts 1500–1550* (vol. 4), hidden among the biblical scenes, grumpy bishops and fragments of daily early-modern life, is a particularly horrifying image. It shows a huge man with an enormous, swollen belly and greasy hair[*] stuffing a child into his mouth, blood and saliva oozing from his lips as the screaming, weeping infant struggles to escape. In a sack dangling from his neck are three more children, another is wedged in the crook of his arm, another hangs underneath, limp, eyes

---

[*]  It is a real testament to the artist – Hans Weiditz – that even in a woodcut you can feel the lank, slimy texture of the figure's hair.

rolled back – dead or unconscious. A final child, its tiny arm clutched in the man's huge hand, defecates in terror. The image was originally printed as a souvenir broadsheet in the early 1500s to be sold at February Carnival in Nuremberg, and is one of many images of a nightmarish monster who, in early modern Germany, was gaining enormous popularity – the child-snatcher, or child-eater. Appearing not just on printed broadsheets but in the Carnival processions themselves, this creature was depicted as a man in a shabby, dark cloak, often with the hood pulled up, and normally with a sack to carry his victims in. His face is smeared with ashes and dirt, and he looks grotesque, filthy, terrifying.

Some broadsheets went into more detail about exactly which children could expect to be eaten. In one, the child-eater is shown waiting at a house with a mother and her weeping son standing in the doorway. Far from protecting the boy, the mother tells him to 'look at the child-devourer', and warns him that the monster goes from house to house, and where he finds children who 'whine' or 'won't be still' he snatches them up after which 'he takes them back to his house and rips them apart, with his teeth he tears them. If you won't be still I will give you to him, therefore be quiet and come inside so he won't find you outside whining.'*

The monster is a threat and a punishment, but despite

---

* I'm not convinced that this strategy would work terribly well – if you want me to whine, show me a cannibalistic monster and tell me that he'll eat me.

the nastiness of warning a child they'll be hurt if they 'whine', there's an element of teasing here as well – no parents were actually handing over the child to a cannibalistic monster. After all, the broadsheets, and the monster himself, were appearing at Carnival – a time of play (albeit unsettling play) rather than punishment. The teasing is perhaps best embodied in a statue on a fountain in the Swiss town of Bern. Sculpted in the 1500s, it shows the child-eater stuffing a child into his unnaturally enormous mouth, with several more children stuffed into a bag at his side. It's hideously unpleasant but painted in bright colours, perched on a pole that shows dancing animals in amusing hats and a favourite of local children. He's fun and scary at the same time, bright, terrifying and frozen in place – able to horrify but not able to attack.

If the carnival monster was a mixture of terror and fun, it may have had its origins in something unequivocally dark. Through the Middle Ages and into the early modern period there had been constant accusations of blood libel against Jewish communities in Europe. This hideous, anti-Semitic idea that Jewish people murdered Christian children to drink their blood had long been prevalent in Europe, and had caused multiple massacres of innocent Jews. Connections were also made between Judaism and the god Saturn – partly because the Jewish Sabbath occurred on Saturn's day (that is, Saturday) every week, and partly because in the Middle Ages Saturn was considered to be a barbaric, evil, monstrous figure – perfect for anti-Semites to correlate with Jewish people. Famously, Saturn also ate his children whole, a monstrous deed that was blended with the blood libel so that in one image of Saturn from the 1400s the god, shoving a child into his mouth, is identified by his hat and badge as Jewish. By the time that the child-killer was stalking the Nuremberg Carnival in the 1500s, though, the association between the child-stealer and Judaism had largely slipped away. The monster may have originated in anti-Semitism, but he was never depicted as Jewish. He was a bogeyman to scare children rather than a deliberately anti-Semitic trope.

We've already seen how Carnival and Christmas blended into each other, and the slipping back of the child-eater from February to early December seems almost inevitable – not only was he a monstrous fancy-dress figure well suited to Christmas guising, he was also the punisher of bad children and it must have felt natural to pair him with St Nicholas, the rewarder of the good. In response, the stories told about St Nicholas began to warp and change to incorporate this child-eating figure – especially the legend of the murdered clerks. Soon, it wasn't a thieving innkeeper who murdered the boys but a starving butcher during a famine who slaughtered them, carved up their bodies, and had begun to pickle them in a vat before Nicholas arrived to save the day – the child-eater stopped in the act. In some regions of France, Belgium and Switzerland the story went that the butcher was forced to work as St Nicholas's assistant to atone for his crimes, punishing the wicked children the saint encountered. Known as Père Fouettard – Father Whipper – he is a dark, hooded figure with a bristling beard. Even though he uses a whip to beat the misbehaving boys and girls, the shadow of murder and cannibalism hangs over him.

In other stories, St Nicholas and the child-killer blended into a single figure. Knecht Ruprecht (or 'Servant Rupert') first appeared in the seventeenth century, in the Christmas parades of Nuremberg (presumably a few weeks later, the townsfolk could have come out to see more child-murdering monsters at the February Carnival). Knecht Ruprecht looks exactly like the child-eater in the early woodcuts, his cloak crumbling, his beard growing ever more wild, his face smeared with ash, a man descending into monster-hood with the trappings of civilisation slipping off him. Like the pop-quizzing St Nicholas of Innsbruck, Knecht Ruprecht questioned his potential victims – one eighteenth-century German engraving shows three children, wringing their hands and looking at the floor as a man in a tall hat with wild hair and a beard raises a finger to them in front of a glowing, glittering Christmas tree. Another younger child, held in its mother's arms behind them, squirms away from the visitation. The image is entitled 'Knecht Ruprecht questions the children'. Knecht Ruprecht would eventually join St Nicholas and become, like Père Fouettard, his threatening assistant rather than his replacement.[*]

In the Rhineland, this figure was known as Belsnickel. He seems to have retained some of the cross-dressing

---

[*] In fact, the Simpsons' dog, 'Santa's Little Helper', is called 'Knecht Ruprecht' in the German.

traditions of the Carnival and guising, at least initially – an early source from the 1830s tells us that he was often portrayed by a man (or a 'veritable woman with masculine force and action') wearing a dress. This figure would bring a switch and a sack of treats to children, throwing the sweets and nuts on the floor and then beating the children's backs as they lunged for them – a game of shrieking laughter as children tried to grab the treats without being hit by the switch. In later iterations the cross-dressing had vanished, and Belsnickel looks like the rest of the child-eaters, with a huge, unruly beard and a dark, dishevelled coat – but still carrying his switch. In the Alsace, meanwhile, the legend attached itself to a real man. Hans von Trotha was a fifteenth-century German nobleman who ended up in a property dispute with the church and found himself excommunicated. Combined with his astonishing two-metre stature, his rejection by the church and subsequent condemnation to damnation led to him becoming a monstrous figure in folklore, a ghastly night wanderer who stalked his old homeland, until by the nineteenth century he was co-opted by St Nicholas to become another dark companion, following the saint with a switch and threatening to beat the children who did not say their prayers.

Where there wasn't a pre-existing figure to adapt as punisher of misbehaving children, one could always be invented. Many guisers – including those guising as Santa's dark helpers, smeared their faces with ashes, likely to make themselves unrecognisable, adding another layer to their disguise. However, by the nineteenth century, this blackening took on a more unpleasant interpretation. Where the representations in the sixteenth century had been anti-Semitic, now at least one author decided to turn the ash-covered faces into blackface. In 1850 a Dutch author wrote the children's book *St Nicholas and His Servant*, in which Santa's malevolent assistant is a Spanish Moor named Piet. Although the name 'Piet' may have been used for a helper of St Nicholas before the book, after its publication Piet became a racist caricature who still – appallingly – appears in Christmas celebrations in the Netherlands.

But alongside the many variations of child-eaters and beaters, there was a whole other breed of monster who came to be associated with St Nicholas – one that had been running across Austria and Bavaria on Epiphany since at least the seventeenth century.

In 1601, in Berchtesgaden, a little Bavarian town about thirty miles from Salzburg, the magistrate issued a ruling that anyone taking part in 'Perchtenlauffen', or 'Perchten run', would be fined. According to the ruling this event was held on 6 January – Epiphany – which likely gave the Perchten run its name; the high German term for Epiphany was *'giperahta naht'*. This was the first of dozens of similar rulings, including another from Berchtesgaden in 1645, which added prison sentences to the punishment, suggesting that no one had been listening to the initial proclamation. In fact, all of these rulings tended to be followed by court cases brought against those who decided to ignore the new laws and go on Perchten runs anyway. Thanks to these rulings and court cases we have some scattered details about what went on. In 1730, the Archbishop of Salzburg mentioned young people dressing up, and bells; another anti-Perchten ruling from 1789 commented that hoods were involved. One report from Kitzbühel in 1735 mentioned young men 'dressed as revolting apparitions with devil masks . . . hung with big bells.' It's clear as well that there was violence – in 1668 a man in Lienz appeared before a court complaining that he had been injured at a Perchten run.

Later sources give far more information – and all of it feels distinctly Krampus-y. By 1908 the monsters of the Salzburg Perchten run were described as wearing black sheepskins and carved masks with long teeth and horns, and sometimes even moveable jaws. Accompanying them were drummers, men with their faces covered by cloth, and two cross-dressing fools (one carrying a distinctly phallic sausage). The whole procession was soundtracked by bells and horns as they went from house to house where they would be offered food and drink. Another account, also from Salzburg, claimed that if different groups met each other they would fight, and that if someone died in the fight wearing a Perchten costume they would need to be buried in secret.* There were

---

\* The exciting, folkloric reason was that anyone wearing a Perchten guise could not be buried as a Christian; the more mundane explanation being that people participating in a banned celebration that had turned deadly might want to hide the evidence.

stories as well of Perchten runners using vaulting poles to evade the authorities, jumping across ditches and vanishing into the night. Many of these accounts were from detractors trying to legislate against the runs, but if only some of their descriptions are true it isn't surprising that people were trying to ban them.

But it wasn't just people ignoring the law who preserved the masked element of the Perchten run. There was another parade on Epiphany in the region, often called the 'beautiful' Perchten run to distinguish itself from the 'ugly' run that was entirely populated with monsters. The beautiful parade involved people wearing elaborate jewelled headdresses and seems, at least in part, to have been a stately procession rather than a wild run. Certainly, the 'beautiful' run was rarely subject to bans, which suggests that it was significantly more restrained than the 'ugly' run. But the 'ugly' still managed to sneak in – not only was there still a fool with a phallic sausage, the performers in headdresses were followed by the shaggy, mask-wearing, horned monsters.

It seems that these traditions grew out of carnival and midwinter celebrations combined – the wild parades of Carnival mingling with the guising and snapping, horned animal heads of Christmas (and of course, the two shared many of the same roots in the first place). At the time of the Perchten runs, Epiphany was more associated with the beginning of Carnival than the end of Christmas, but as St Nicholas took on more monstrous assistants (who also had their origins in Carnival), the monsters of the Perchten parades must have seemed like obvious sidekicks for the saint. They began to slip backwards to early December and started obeying St Nicholas and punishing wicked children rather than just causing general chaos. When the Bishop of Salzburg complained, in 1740, about the 'bad habit of transferring pre-Lenten traditions to the time before the church holidays of Christmas, New Year's, and Epiphany' – he might have been talking about the appearances on St Nicholas's night of the child-eaters or the Perchten monsters, or both.* In the joyous confusion of folklore, the Perchten run survived on Epiphany as well. In Austria today, on 6 January, parades with elaborate, enormous headdresses can still be seen – along with a group of demons clustering behind and looking a little lost without their saint.

In many local celebrations, the monsters took the name 'Perchten' with them even after their connection with Epiphany had been lost, and the term began to apply to the monsters themselves rather than the day they used to run through the streets. In other places, different names may already have been associated with the creatures at Epiphany, or developed as they became linked with St Nicholas. The reasoning behind most of the names is lost in time, but Ganggerls, Perchtens and

---

* Some of the creatures stayed associated with Carnival, and there are monsters in Alpine carnival traditions – like the Tschaggata in Switzerland and the Pschuurirolli in the Rhinewald – who look exactly like Krampuses, with pelts, horns and cowbells, but who have no association with Christmas. It's also notable that Krampus masks are still called 'Larven', a term that typically refers to carnival masks.

Toifis proliferated throughout the region. It was only in the late 1800s and early 1900s that Krampus (perhaps coming from the German word for claw – *'kralle'*) came to dominate.

Overlooking the Salzburg Christkindlmarkt, tucked away in the corner next to an ice rink and cafe, is the Christmas Museum. It's small but full of treasures – nineteenth-century playsets of Christmas market stalls crammed with their own, tiny, glittering baubles; decorations made in the 1920s from bright shards of glass; antique children's books of Christmas stories – and case after case of Krampuses. There are the expected Krampus masks, but what might be more surprising is the enormous quantity of late nineteenth- and twentieth-century Krampus-themed merch: ceramic pepper pots in the shape of the monster; little jars with his head popping out of the top; porcelain dolls of Krampus with sacks and baskets that were made to be stuffed with nuts and sweets before they were given as gifts. There are little art-deco metal figurines (a rare entry in the 'tasteful' category of Krampus tat), Krampus gingerbread and chocolate moulds, and a heart-shaped confectioner's box with a bit of brown fur stuck to the top in the shape of a Krampus head, complete with miniature chains dripping from his horns. In one display, a debonair Krampus doll wearing a black-and-red lounge suit lazes on a sofa; in another a golden walnut opens to reveal a tiny St Nicholas and Krampus standing together. Heartbreakingly for those of us who long to own a Krampus pepper pot none of this is available in the museum shop, which only has a small row of Krampus baubles and some postcards. The best the markets outside can do is some *lebkuchen* or ginger-bread stamped with his picture.

Oddly enough, the era of Krampus mania that inspired all of this Krampus junk began with the postcard, which was itself a novel form of correspondence, first accepted in Europe by the Austro-Hungarian post office in 1869.[*] Cards featuring a Christmas monster proved an imme-diately popular way of sending seasonal greetings. Lying in a case in the centre of the main 'Krampus' room of the Salzburg museum is a typical example – a small postcard showing a stylish woman dressed in red leggings, a red cape, and a red cap. She might have wandered in from any early twentieth-century fashion magazine, except that in her hands she holds an enormous switch of birch branches, and growing from her cap are two delicate black horns. Next to her is the text 'Gruss vom Krampus' – 'Greetings from Krampus'. There is a whole subgenre of 'sexy' Krampus cards, which often feature a giant, scantily dressed lady Krampus whipping grown men. But there are hundreds of other themes, too; some showing the monster beating children, stalking them through the

---

[*]    In fact, the first ever postcard was technically sent in the UK in 1840 (long before they were widely accepted by the postal service) and was done as a joke. It was hand drawn, mailed by and addressed to the practical joker, Theodore Hook, and featured caricatures of postal workers, which would have been seen by the actual postal workers who processed it.

snowy countryside, or chasing adult victims. In Vienna, where the postcard fad took off, the most common name for the Christmas monster was Krampus, and so this was the name used on the cards, the name which spread far and wide, gradually ousting all the other monsters. So, if you're wondering why Perchtens, Klaubaufs and all the rest of horned Christmas monsters often get lumped in with Krampuses, why I went to a Krampus run in Salzburg rather than a Perchten run, and why the 2015 horror film was called *Krampus* and not *Ganggerl*, the postcard craze is the answer. Becoming a light-hearted joke might be a strange fate for a monster – except that the teasing element was always present in the Krampuses and their brothers, even when they were rampaging violently through the streets or devouring little children.

A few days after the Krampus run, I watch my niece excitedly writing her letter to Santa, trying desperately to read her handwriting over her shoulder so I can bring her at least one of the things she's asked for. Sitting in a warm, bright kitchen and watching a child fully embrace the magic that comes with Father Christmas, I find myself glad that Krampus has no part in her Christmas mythology, that she has no knowledge or fear of any dark helpers. But then, as she finishes her message, she starts assuring her parents that she's been good this year – that Santa has no reason to withhold her presents – and I realise that her Santa has a mean streak, a nastiness I'm not sure I like. Krampus, to many, can feel too sinister for the festive season – a figure who stands in hideous opposition to the jolly Father Christmas. But it seems to me that the threatening monsters enhance these friendlier legends. By taking on the task of punishing children, Krampus allows Santa to be imbued only with the bright magic, and by being a monster with such a terrifying mythology the punishments themselves are no longer a petty lack of gifts, but horrifyingly exciting – the sinister darkness that lurks in the shadows of every good fairy tale. In fact, even in places without any of the older dark helpers of Santa, we seem to realise that something is missing from the stories. Invented in 2005, the Elf on the Shelf has become enormously popular, spreading throughout the US and UK – a punisher who skulks in a child's home through Advent, spying on them and taking note of their misdeeds, a horrible, creepy little figure who, like Krampus, allows Santa to rise above the fray.

In Salzburg I catch sight of a Krampus at a Christmas market prowling under a glittering tree, and watch as he stalks his prey – a small child trying to persuade his mother to buy him sweets. Perhaps it's just that I've spent too long immersed in the darkness of the season, but to me at least, there's no contradiction between the glittering fairy lights and the horned, shaggy monster. In a world of snow and Christmas magic, he looks right at home.

# FIVE

# The Christmas Witches

## Lucy's Night
## 13 December

By 13 December in Finland there are eighteen hours of freezing darkness each day. When the sun does finally appear it's pale and low in the sky – even midday feels like a grey twilight and by 6pm, when I arrive at the white, domed cathedral in the centre of Helsinki, it's already been night for close to three hours. It's been snowing for the last two days, and the harbour, just visible from the top of the cathedral steps, is completely frozen over – it looks like you could walk to the little island of Valkosaari, about a mile out, over the sheet of ice. The darkness and the cold are immense and oppressive, and even though I'm part of a huge crowd, gathered on the steep steps of the cathedral and the square around it, it feels like we're huddled together, hunkering down against the night.

## The Dead of Winter

Tonight is St Lucy's Night – barely noted in much of Europe, but an important saint's day in the Nordic countries, not to mention a vital part of the Christmas celebrations. There's even a bun (all good festivals come with their own baked goods) – a *lucia-pullat*, or Lucy bun. On my walk to the cathedral I stopped at a bakery to buy one – a curled twist of dough tasting of sweet saffron and studded with raisins, the grassiness of the saffron a touch of spring even in the depths of winter. As I finish the last few bites I find a place to stand on the cathedral steps, and wait – in the darkness, in the cold, the snow piling up around my feet. I've been there for around half an hour,[*] when, suddenly, a spotlight is switched on over the cathedral door, flooding the square in brilliant white light so bright it feels stronger than the sun has been in weeks. The door to the cathedral opens and a beautiful girl steps outside, wearing a robe of white furs bound by a red sash around her waist. On her head she wears a wreath of lit candles – a magnificent, glowing crown. Shining in the spotlight she seems like a personification of light itself, and in many ways she is. She's dressed as St Lucy, who, with her saint's day in the depths of winter and a name derived from the Latin word for light, has come to be thought of not just as a saint, but as the light coming back into the winter darkness.[†]

---

[*] All the while becoming increasingly aware that my boots are not as waterproof as I thought they were.

[†] This connection was helped by the fact that, in the Gregorian

For the last hour, inside the cathedral, there has been a service commemorating her, telling her legends and singing her hymns – and crowning the girl selected to be this year's Lucy with her wreath of candles. Standing in the cathedral portico, she beams, waving to the assembled crowd. She's followed by a parade of more young women, all wearing white robes, all carrying candles, all smiling the same serene smiles. Wreathed in glimmering light in this endless winter night, they seem unearthly – a glorious, solemn vision. Behind them is a gaggle of boys wearing pointed cardboard hats and carrying wonky stars decorated with tinsel. They look like they've accidentally wandered into a divine visitation on their way to a school nativity play.

Slowly, St Lucy descends the steps, which have been decorated with flaming torches. Next to her purity and whiteness (helped by the fact that the candles on her head and held by her fellows are all LED), the orange of the firelight looks almost dirty. At the bottom of the stairs, in front of a gigantic Christmas tree, is a white, icy throne, perched on the back of a slightly incongruous parade float. She climbs in and it pulls away at a walking pace followed by her parade of white-dressed girls and boys, a glowing beacon that weaves its way through the crowds. I wait until they're out of sight, the spotlight over the cathedral

---

calendar, 13 December was actually the date of midwinter. In fact, on the current midwinter in the Nordics there are still some St Lucy celebrations, a memory of when her day and the longest night of the year coincided.

door turned off, the square plunged back into darkness. St Lucy does not stop smiling or waving the entire time.

Lucy ceremonies like this take place across the Nordic countries, some just as magnificent, others far more lowkey. The ceremonies started in the 1930s in Sweden, but the tradition of girls dressing as Lucy with a crown of candles and a white robe (normally to serve a breakfast of Lucy buns to the household) dates back to at least the nineteenth century. St Lucy herself, of course, is far older. According to her myths she was a young Christian girl living in Syracuse in the fourth century AD who turned down a suitor because she had promised her virginity to God and wished to give her dowry to the poor. One of her good deeds was bringing food and water to the Christians who had been forced to hide in the city's catacombs because of the governor's religious persecution. Lucy – according to the story – needed a light to find her way in the darkness, but in order to free up her hands so she could bring as many provisions as possible she wore a wreath of candles on her head as a kind of prototype head-torch.[*] Eventually she was martyred, in some accounts, by having her eyes gouged out,[†] murdered

---

[*] This is a fairly late addition to the myth, and likely came when the image of St Lucy merged with that of the German and Austrian Chriskindl – a representation of the infant Jesus who appears at Christmas, and is portrayed by a young girl with candles on her head, dressed all in white.

[†] This has led to a series of darkly bizarre medieval images in which she's shown carrying her eyeballs on a gruesome little cake-stand.

by the Christianity-hating governor when her rejected suitor reported her religion to the authorities.

It's only eight days since the Krampus run, and there's something in the serene beauty of Lucy's Night that feels much more uncomfortable than the prowling demons: the girls smiling and mute, paragons of a type of female modesty, piety and self-sacrifice that comes with a lot of associations more troubling than any goat-monster could conjure.* But there's another aspect to all this, one far more suited to Krampus (and me). My Finnish hosts have already told me a different story of Lucy – that her hated suitor claimed her eyes were the most beautiful in the world, so she gouged them out and sent them to him, pointing out that now he had her eyes he could leave her alone. The story is clearly a play on the legends of her losing her eyes in her martyrdom, but twisted into a delightfully nasty little fairy story. It's telling, as well, that while most saints have a saint's day, Lucy has her night.

As I drift away from the cathedral with the rest of the crowd, I stop off at the bakery and buy another bun. I don't eat this one – instead, when I get back to my room, I lay it on top of its paper bag on my bedside table. As an

---

* It's unsurprising to learn that Lucy is often held up as a symbol of the kind of regressive conservatism that has led to outpourings of hatred at the mere suggestion that she should be represented by anyone other than a white girl – and that's before even considering whether women and girls really need any more messaging about the importance of beauty, purity, and how they should martyr themselves for others.

additional precaution I don't write a single word, tucking my laptop into its case and leaving it on a chair on the other side of the room, out of temptation's reach. Lucy has another side to her, and working when you should be celebrating in her name is to invite her wrath, as is failing to leave out an offering of food for her and her companions.*

This other Lucy is nothing like the demure, sweet victim of the hagiographies or the pure, white vision I've just seen outside the cathedral. Instead, on 13 December, she is said to ride through the skies with a cavalcade of the dead, of ghosts and, sometimes, of children who died while still unbaptised. Going house to house with her terrifying entourage, she looks for the food that has been left out for her. If all is well, she'll eat the offerings and bring good fortune in return, and if she encounters any good children on her way she gives them treats. But if the food offerings are incorrect or forgotten, and if Lucy finds that the tasks of the household – especially those related to weaving – have not been finished and laid aside for her celebration, she brings disorder, bad luck and death. If she finds children who have misbehaved, she'll gut them, pull out their organs, stuff them full of straw, and sew them back up again. Sometimes she's depicted holding a distaff with a child's intestines

---

* I'm hoping that Lucy doesn't take the view that my entire trip out to Finland to learn about her could technically be counted as work, and that she didn't see me scribbling notes during her parade.

twined around it, an impressive combining of the normally very separate interests of cloth-making and disembowelling. Inevitably for a Christmas monster, guisers used to dress as Lucy, going house to house veiled and wrapped in white sheets, holding knives and empty bowls which they cry to be filled with blood and guts. Hideous, haggish and often sporting an enormous nose (sometimes represented as a cone that covers her face entirely, so she looks like a creature from a Dr Seuss-based nightmare), this is a Lucy you wouldn't want turning up if you were hiding in some catacombs (although she might not feel entirely out of place). But from the warmth of my bed, with my food offering safely laid out, I prefer Lucy knowing she has darkness in her as well as light.

I'm not the only one who prefers the monster – the other Lucy is celebrated well beyond the Nordic countries, finding her way into Bavarian and Austrian tradition where she is known as *schiache Luz* – bad Lucy – and *bluadige Luz* – bloody Lucy. Look into Bavarian and Austrian tradition further and there is another witch monster who bears a striking similarity to Lucy: Perchta. Rather than travelling on Lucy's Night, Perchta conducts her grim business on the Twelve Nights of Christmas or the week after Lucy's Night (a period known as the Christmas Ember Days), and is especially associated with Epiphany itself. In fact, it's where Perchta's name likely comes from – and why it sounds so similar to the 'Perchten' monsters mentioned in the chapter before – both were named after the day they appeared.* But in all other regards, Lucy and Perchta are almost identical – rewarding good children and gutting the bad before stuffing them with straw (Perchta adds the flourish of sewing up her victims using a ploughshare as a needle and a chain as thread); obsessed with the idea that the tasks of the household – especially weaving – must be completed and set aside before their nights begin, and demanding food offerings be left out for them, bringing good luck where they find them and bad where they do not.†

There's another Christmas witch too – though an altogether kinder one – the Befana. An Italian variant, Befana, like Perchta, appears on Epiphany, and, like Perchta, she takes her name from the festival. She also gives good children sweets, but the bad children who meet Befana only have to contend with gifts of coal rather than being gutted.

The history of these Christmas witches may well be one of the most complex of all the seasonal monsters. After all, only an utter mess of tangling beliefs can lead to a semi-benevolent, disembowelling witch who demands offerings, gives presents, and flies across the land followed by an army of the dead.

---

\* In recent years, the similarity in the names had led to a blending of the traditions, so that slightly confused Perchta witches turn up at the Perchten runs.

† I actually met a Perchta in Salzburg: she was parading with the Krampuses, looking every inch the stereotypical witch, with a broomstick, dishevelled wig, and enormous fake nose.

One of the first references to the Christmas witch, or at least, to her predecessors, comes from the early eleventh century, when Burchard, Bishop of the city of Worms in Germany, wrote an unimpressed list of common beliefs no good Christian should have (along with the appropriate penances for holding them),* including:

> Have you believed or participated in this infidelity, that some wicked women, turned back after Satan, seduced by illusions and phantoms of demons believe and affirm: that with Diana, the goddess of the pagans, and an unnumbered multitude of women, they ride on certain beasts and traverse many areas of the earth in the stillness of the quiet night.[1]

This isn't the only mention Burchard made of women riding out at night in a host led by a goddess – of his two hundred or so rules, it's the subject of four. And numerous other medieval churchmen complained about this idea as well as Burchard, a collection of angry fragments that suggests it was a commonly held belief, no matter how much the church might have tried to stamp it out.

---

* Of course, we've encountered Burchard before – one of the other non-Christian practices he was grumpy about was people dressing up as stags on 1 January. It's also worth saying that Burchard was likely copying the bulk of his rules from an earlier document, dating from the tenth century.

Sometimes the goddess leading the women is called Holda or Herodias, not Diana. Sometimes the women are able to pass through closed doors to sneak away in spirit, leaving their bodies lying in bed with their husbands while their souls cavort through the night. Sometimes, they eat children. And sometimes, they devour people's organs, and stuff them with straw.

These night-travelling women seem, in part, to be based on Roman ideas around witchcraft. In Rome, in the second half of the first century BC, a general idea that women were more likely than men to use magic merged with female monsters called '*striga*' – screeching demonesses who flew about at night in packs, ate the organs of children, and stuffed them with straw. Soon, Roman witches were not just female magic users but night-flying, cannibalistic, baby-murdering monsters who crammed straw into their victims. We can even follow the popular belief in cannibalistic strigas through Late Antiquity – from about AD 500 on, Christian kings were writing law codes that made it illegal to accuse women of being strigas and eating other people's organs. Just to connect the two as clearly as possible, at one point Burchard even calls his night-women 'striga' – and, just like the early Christian kings, his rules are not against *being* a striga, they're against believing that strigas exist at all.*

---

* This might be surprising, given how gung-ho the Church would be about persecuting witches in the early modern period, but a lot of things changed over the centuries that separated Burchard from the witch-hunters. In fact, the authors of the infamous witch-hunting

But Burchard's women were not completely monstrous. Although the bishop keeps telling us that the whole thing is an illusion conjured by demons, the phenomenon he's describing seems to have appealed to at least some people. Women – real women – seemed to want to be associated with these groups, and were claiming happily that they had ridden out in the night with Holda and Diana. It is a dream of power, of freedom, but not – quite – of evil; even the child-murdering and disembowelling doesn't stick. In ancient Rome, if a witch ate your heart and stuffed you with straw you might live long enough to die ironically the next morning, but you wouldn't expect to lead a long and happy life with grass instead of organs. The victims of the night-travelling women, on the other hand, are genuinely 'made alive again', while children murdered by them are restored, unharmed, to their cribs by morning.

The goddesses said to lead the night ride also give the outing a more ambiguous feel. The name Diana can probably be dismissed – medieval clergymen used it as a catch-all name for any magical woman who wasn't directly Christian, whether or not the woman in question had anything to do with hunting or the moon (perhaps because Diana is the only pagan goddess whose name appears in the Bible). Herodias, meanwhile, is a figure

tract *Malleus Maleficarum* wrestled with these early denials of striga-witches, while churchmen who opposed the witch hunts would often refer back to these earlier texts in an attempt to rein in their murderous colleagues.

who lived very much in grey areas, at least in medieval folklore. In the Bible she's the wife of King Herod, but in stories told in the Middle Ages she was his daughter, who fell in love with John the Baptist. When her father found out, he ordered the saint beheaded. Herodias went to kiss the severed head, but John the Baptist (who had never returned her love, and was presumably unimpressed by how the entire mess has turned out for him) blew her away, up into the sky, where she spent the rest of eternity dancing and parading through the night – an obvious figure to lead other women in the darkness, and one who, though connected to plenty of evil deeds, was not evil herself. 'Holda' is even more positive. Her name seems to relate to an early German word *huld* – which means 'friendly' or 'gracious' – hardly a quality you'd associate with murderous bands of monsters.

The likely explanation for this positivity is that the striga-witches were blending in with another group of female night-travellers in medieval folklore – ones who brought abundance and prosperity: the Fates.

Again, Burchard's list of penances is a showcase for these folkloric female figures:

> Have you prepared the table in your house and set on the table your food and drink, with three knives, that if those three sisters whom past generations and old-time foolishness called the Fates should come, they may take refreshment there?[2]

According to Burchard, the belief held that once the Fates had eaten from your table, they would help 'either now or in the future'. The practice he's referencing seems to relate to a common early medieval tradition of leaving out food for a group of women who travelled by night, and who would bring prosperity in return. Often led by a figure called Satia or Abundia (names meaning 'Satisfaction' and 'Abundance' in Latin – a set that 'Holda' fits right into), or generically referred to as 'The Good Ladies', they went to homes at night, consuming the offerings that had been left out for them and bringing good luck in return. It's worth noting as well that their 'consumption' is magical – anything they eat returns untouched in the morning, much like the devoured children and organs consumed by the night-travelling strigas.

It's unclear where exactly this tradition came from – there was a goddess of plenty called Abundantia in ancient Rome, and there were three women who personified the Fates, but no one was setting the table for any of them. Nor was there any suggestion that the Fates could be bribed with food offerings in the ancient world. It looks instead like these practices developed in the early Middle Ages – and were almost immediately absorbed into the striga mythology, lending them positive attributes that are otherwise difficult to explain when it comes to infant-eating night travellers. When Burchard was writing in the eleventh century, the two mythologies are sat just slightly apart – the striga-women were taking on ambiguous elements, but no one was setting the table for them, and the Fates are mentioned in an entirely different rule.\* By the thirteenth century at the latest, the two had collapsed into each other and people were leaving out food for a figure variously called Holda, Holle, Herodias, Diana, Satia or Abundia who led groups of mortal women to roam the night, slipping into locked houses to drink, party and feast – while also eating children and organs and stuffing people with straw (and then restoring them to life for the morning).

It may also have been The Good Ladies who brought Christmas into all of this. Burchard doesn't specify when his Fates came visiting, but he does mention that people only left out food offerings 'at certain times of the year', which is both extremely tantalising and pro-foundly unhelpful of him.† It would make sense if they were linked – not only do they give and receive gifts – a very Christmassy activity – but New Year would be a time when people were looking forward to the year ahead and hoping for the kind of prosperity and good fortune the Ladies might bring. And of course, the night-travelling women also went house to house, demanding food and drink – an activity that, thanks to the guisers, was

---

\* It's possible that this association between the ever-weaving Fates and these groups of night women is what brought weaving to the Christmas witches – but it's also possible that, as a task normally performed by women, weaving was felt to be a suitable interest for witch monsters who led groups of women at night.

† As an aside: Burchard, we know you knew how to write a date, because you specifically complained about masking on 1 January. Would it have killed you to write the actual dates the Fates sup-posedly appeared as well?

extremely Christmas-coded. With Christmas's association with death and demons, it's also likely that the more monstrous elements of the tradition helped to link it to Christmas.

However it happened, by the early thirteenth century the connections between the Good Ladies, the striga-women and Christmas were fixed, with one text claiming that:

> On the night of Christ's Nativity they set the table for the Queen of Heaven, whom people call Frau Holda, that she might help them.[3]

In the fourteenth century, the name Perchta started being used to refer to these women. With the name derived from the word 'Epiphany', it may be that Perchta herself was part of a medieval tradition of personifying festivals. From the early fourteenth century on, over the Twelve Nights of Christmas Perchtas joined the gang, roaming about at night, bringing prosperity to those who left them food, occasionally eating babies, disembowelling people and stuffing them with straw. St Lucy, sweet, innocent and pure, would be absorbed into all of this as well – a girl associated with Christmas and midwinter because of the date of her saint's day, pulled into the pack of semi-benevolent monstrous Christmas women.

But in medieval folklore there was a third group of people prowling through the night (was anyone in the Middle Ages getting any sleep?), and they brought one final attribute to the Christmas witch. After all, in the fourteenth century Perchta was leading bands of women on her night travels, but by the early modern period she was leading a procession of the dead – and how they got involved with the flying witches takes even more untangling.

In the early eleventh century AD, a monk called Orderic Vitalis recorded a tale that had been told to him by a young priest, Walchelin. Returning from a sick call late at night, the priest had heard what he thought sounded like an approaching army. Taking shelter between four medlar trees he watched as the group approached, and saw to his horror that it was not a living army but a procession of the dead, all being punished for the sins they had committed while they were alive. Passing by his hiding place, Walchelin saw thieves forced to tote impossibly heavy sacks of their ill-gotten loot, a murderer whipped by demons, 'lecherous' women on saddles made of nails, plenty of badly behaved knights – even a segment of corrupt churchmen, which caused Orderic to muse that while men faultily judge from external appearances of goodness, God knows better.[*] This is the first attestation

---

[*] Orderic even names some of these sinful churchmen, who seem to have been Walchelin's contemporaries, including one Hugh, Bishop of Lisieux. There's no suggestion of why the author might have felt he deserved to be included in the cavalcade (and Orderic even wrote nice things about him at some other points) – but his modern reputation is as a man who thought he was helping to reform the Church and sat on a council that tried to stamp out corruption – but since

we have of a group of the dead parading through the night, and, according to Orderic, like all good monsters, they had a fondness for Christmastime – Walchelin stumbled across them on 1 January.

What's markedly less easy to understand is where the folklore behind the parade of the dead originated. While Orderic's is the first account of it, there's a hint that he wasn't the originator of the belief. As Walchelin stares in wonder at the dead, he identifies them as 'part of Herlechin's rabble'. A few decades after Orderic was writing, we have another source on Herlechin – Walter Map. In his book *Trifles of Courtiers*, he gave a detailed account of how 'Herlequin' was a great king of England, who, along with all of his knights, attended the wedding of a strange lord. As Herlequin and his men mounted up to leave the festivities a little dog leapt into Herlequin's lap, and their host told them that they should not dismount before the dog did. When they returned home the dog refused to get down – and when some of the knights decided to ignore the warning they vanished into dust as soon as their feet touched the ground. Cursed to wander forever, Herlequin and his knights – according to Walter Map – travel the land, not quite living, not quite dead, with a little dog still sitting on the lap of their leader. Now, this is markedly different from Orderic's account,

---

he came from an extremely wealthy, influential family, his 'reforming' was often severely compromised as he tried to protect his own interests. Living in 2024, I'm fine saying that sort of behaviour is worth at least a few years processing with the tormented dead.

and has led to suggestions that Orderic had intentionally taken a pagan myth and Christianity-ed it up with all his talk of punishments and devils of hell. That's a tempting thought – but there's no reference to Herlequin before Orderic (and plenty of places where we'd expect it to be mentioned if it truly was a well-known pre-Christian legend – like all those churchmen listing un-Christian popular beliefs). Even more confusingly, Walter Map tells another story in the same book where Herlequin appears leading a parade of the dead exactly like the one described by Orderic – clearly, even in the Middle Ages no one was quite sure what was going on.*

However, it does seem likely that whatever was happening with this little mess of myths, it all originated around the time that Orderic was writing, rather than being some ancient and long-held belief that was just never mentioned in any sources. This is partly because we have plenty of places we'd expect to see references to Herlequin and his hordes prior to the eleventh century, but neither his name nor the folklore of roving bands of the dead (or even roving bands of anyone, apart from the strigas and the Good Ladies) ever appear, and partly because the whole tradition seems to reflect concerns specific to this period in time. When Orderic was

---

* A little after Map, another medieval author decided to try and puzzle this all out for himself, wondering if the mysterious night-travelling groups that were reportedly crossing the lands were the punished dead, or ghosts, or demons, and, after much consideration, came to the conclusion that he had no idea at all.

writing, there was an increasing interest in what happened to the Christian dead. Obviously, everyone was waiting for the inevitable Judgement Day, but with the Day itself still not in the calendar even after a thousand years of Christianity there were more stories about, and interest in, what happened after death in the meantime. Ideas of purgatory, especially, were popular in this period (it was in 1274 that the Church got around to defining purgatory for the first time) and a parade of the dead being punished for their lifetime's sins would slot in perfectly.

It's easy to see how the Christmassy night-travelling dead combined with the Christmassy night-travelling witches – especially given that the witches tended to go about with an entourage. From the late Middle Ages on, the Christmas witch was as likely to be followed by a parade of the dead as a parade of women. And the legends of this cavalcade became part of the folklore for what would later be called the 'Wild Hunt'. In some places, Odin would take over from the witches to lead the dead, in others there would be werewolves mixed in with the group. Sometimes it was an army that crossed the land; sometimes ghostly hunters chasing a white stag. But even in cases where Odin took over from the witches, the Hunt often remained tied to Christmas. In fact, there's a Christmas tradition in some parts of Germany and Austria that washing shouldn't be hung out over Christmas, lest the Wild Hunt become entangled in it, and that windows should be left open at night to allow the Hunt to pass through.

*The Dead of Winter*

As I settle down to sleep on St Lucy's Night, I eye up the window in my warm little bedroom. I'm staying with family friends a little way out of Helsinki, in a village surrounded by forest. Outside, the snow is still falling thickly among the shadows of the trees – an untamed Christmas wonderland. If an undead horde wanted to pass through, they wouldn't look out of place in the darkness and the storm. I briefly consider trying the window latch, but decide that letting snow pile up inside the house and allowing in all that cold air wouldn't be the best way to show gratitude to my hosts. Besides, having only one window open is surely an invitation for disaster, giving the Hunt an entrance but no exit. Reluctantly, I leave the latch be – but I keep watch on the window until I fall asleep, on the snow, still falling, on the moon fighting its way through the clouds.

In recent years, the figure of the witch has become something of a feminist icon, and it's wonderful to discover that we are not the first to delight in the witch's subversion of conventional femininity, that for a short period a thousand years ago women dreamt of powerful nights spent running free, revelling in the darkness with a gang of other women, drinking, carousing, maybe even murdering, all while it seemed they were asleep next to their husbands. But then, in the early modern period, the context of the Christmas witches changed completely as the Inquisition kicked off witch hunts. Desperate to prove that witches were heretics (and so bring them under their jurisdiction), the witch hunters claimed that the night rides with strigas and the Good Women were actually satanic rituals, led not by goddesses but by the devil himself, with the babies eaten and stuffed with straw no longer magically made whole in the morning. Women confessed to night flights and wild revels, only to be tortured into 'admitting' that they were also having sex with the devil and devouring infants, often over the Christmas period. In 1457, just before the witch trials really got underway, in the valley of Fassa in the South Tyrol three women confessed to nocturnal dancing with 'The Good Ladies' during the Ember Days. The women were lucky that the true witch panic had yet to begin – they were found guilty, but their lives were spared. Only fifty years later, and around ten miles away, a man named Giovanni delle Piatte claimed he had met Herodias, after which he feasted and flew around the world over Christmas. Giovanni managed to avoid any worse punishment than banishment – by accusing fourteen other 'witches' of having been there with him. Holda, Perchta, Herodias, and the witches travelling to dark revels in packs, all ran through witchcraft trials.

This Christmassy bent to the witchcraft trials may also be why werewolves were commonly perceived as being more likely to turn over Christmas. Werewolves and witches were tied together in the early modern period, with a lesser-known subset of the witch trials being, in actuality, werewolf trials. In one trial, in Livonia in the 1600s, an old man claimed he turned into a werewolf on St Lucy's Night. In the sixteenth century, the

Archbishop of Sweden even recorded a legend where, over the Twelve Nights of Christmas:

> There is a gathering of a huge multitude of wolves, which have been changed from men, and which during that night rage with such fierceness ... that the inhabitants suffer more hurt from them than they ever do from natural wolves, for these human wolves break down doors ... and descend into cellars where they drink out whole tuns of beer of mead.[4]

Here the werewolves are behaving almost exactly like the Christmas witches and their rampaging, revelling hordes – except that there's no suggestion that the beer and mead might be replenished come dawn. They also sound astonishingly similar to the packs of masked guisers roaming the countryside every Christmas, demanding food and drink from the houses they visited.

There are few modern commemorations of the Christmas werewolves,* but across Alpine towns, every Christmas, witches are still burned in effigy – a memory of the Christmas trials. On 2 January, in the North Italian town of Cavalese, the transcripts from witch trials are read aloud before four stuffed figures, tied to stakes, are set on fire – a solemn, awful ceremony that commemorates the horrors of the witch hunts. In other places,

---

* There was a small statue to the Livonian werewolves erected in Chicago in the 1990s – which was then, appallingly, destroyed in 2019 due to 'miscommunications' with renovators.

though, the vibe is different. In the Lombardy town of Guissano, huge figures of witches are dragged through the town to a jaunty drum-beat before they're burned by a baying crowd. These figures represent real women who were murdered out of hatred, misogyny and ignorance, their effigies paraded to upbeat music and set aflame while people cheer wildly, hideous deaths enacted and re-enacted year on year, celebrated again and again. Of all the monstrous Christmas traditions, this is one I have no wish to attend.

But even as the stories of the Christmas witches were twisted to become something horrifying, turned into accusations of Witches' Sabbaths and actual child murder, into lies that could be used to justify centuries of misogynistic torment and death, the Perchtas, Lucys and Holdas retained their old ways, their old legends. After all, you couldn't persecute a fabled witch, so the inquisitors didn't bother reshaping them, and their stories kept the same, older, patterns. The children were still stuffed with straw (something broadly lost in the witchcraft trials, where women tended to be accused of eating children outright or casting spells that led to their deaths) and still allowed to live again come morning. The Christmas witches themselves remained powerful and benevolent (if treated correctly), retained their wild night rights, their entourages, their offerings, ready to appear anew each Christmas, to remind us of the dreams of freedom and power that were perverted by the witch trials.

There was one final shift for the Christmas witches to undergo. In the eighteenth century, the witch trials were winding down and genuine fear of witches was fading. The Christmas witches, taking a nod from the other Christmas monsters of the time (and presumably encouraged by the fact that they'd always been interested in devouring infants and bringing terror to those who'd committed infractions against them) started to focus their attentions solely on naughty children. In one woodcut from 1750 Perchta appears as 'Butzen-Bercht' – 'bogey-Percht' – every inch the Nuremburg child-snatcher. She has on her back a basket stuffed with children and is towering over a group of girls, the text underneath claiming that if she encounters lazy children she will 'reel the intestines out of your belly, and fill the hole with woodshavings'. Befana, meanwhile started to emerge as a less murderous variant in Italy – less likely to gut anyone, but still insisting that children needed to be good.

There was another ghastly Christmas woman who was also punishing children by the eighteenth century: Grýla, the Icelandic ogress we have already met as a guising monster. She may have been attested as early as the thirteenth century but by the seventeenth century, she was shifting, starting to focus her attentions on naughty children – normally popping them into her giant stew to cook and eat, and often helped by her Yule Lads – 13 horrible, mischievous young boys. Using Grýla to scare children was so prolific that it was condemned in the 1746 Icelandic Decree for House

Discipline.* Perhaps it was her growing witchiness – her propensity to cook and eat little children at Christmastime – that led to her being associated with another Christmas monster in Iceland, the Yule Cat. This giant, terrible cat is said to eat anyone who doesn't have new clothes for Christmas and is first recorded in sources in the nineteenth century. Its origins are unclear, though it was perhaps a variant of Christmas animal guises. It was certainly not connected with Grýla initially, but by the mid-twentieth century they were linked – perhaps a terrifying cat seemed a natural familiar for a witch-like figure.

As I fell asleep on 13 December in Finland, I had hoped Lucy would be pleased enough with her bun that she let me join her to ride through the darkness and snow on her wild revels, eating and drinking, rewarding the good and punishing the bad. But I sleep through until morning, and if I have any dreams I don't remember them. The bun is still there on the bedside table, the paper bag it's sitting on turned glossy and see-through with grease. Though of course, that doesn't mean Lucy hasn't been, hasn't eaten it and then returned it to its place, ready for me to eat it again for breakfast.

---

* Don't go thinking that this was a progressive piece of legislation that protected children, by the way – it was primarily concerned with ensuring parents themselves were legally obligated to punish children who misbehaved.

# SIX

# Old Gods

## *The Stonehenge Solstice*
## *22 December*

Behind every tale of Christmas monsters lurks the true darkness of Christmas – the solstice, and the longest night of the year. No matter how brightly our fires burn, or how many fairy lights we turn on, Christmas is still spent deep in the shadows. As I walk across the Salisbury plains in the pre-dawn darkness on the morning of 22 December, the night that is thinning around me is the longest of the year, finally reaching its end. On the roads up to the horizon I can see the white-and-red headlights and tail lights of cars that are completely stationary, so great is the flood of people arriving. In fact, I've had to abandon my car (and its driver) to walk, weaving among the stopped vehicles, joined by others who've done the same, so there are hundreds, then thousands of us walking together, turning off the road and onto smaller paths, tramping in the mud over the fields, until as the sky begins to lighten, we can see the strange, huge, hulk of Stonehenge standing in front of us.

We cross the shallow ditch that surrounds the monument,* and then head through the well-known ring of stone archways, each made from two huge vertical stones with a third laid horizontally on top – an arrangement called a 'trilithon'. Within the outer ring are more trilithons, freestanding but arranged in a semicircle, and standing taller than the ones in the outer circle. Close to, their surfaces are rough and deeply embedded with lichen, but still, when the light is just right, glittering – tiny crystals of quartz catching the first light of dawn, glinting from the rock. It is incredible to be among them, to see how huge they are when you're standing in their centre, how strangely they still sit in the landscape, despite having weathered here for five thousand years.

With me is a glorious assortment of people – druids, women in flower crowns, a man wearing only a tank top with blue paint smeared across his body, someone dressed as a pterodactyl. For some, this is one of the most important days on their religious calendar, for others it's a bit of early morning Christmas fun. For many, it's a spiritual experience – I see plenty of people slip off their gloves and run their hands over the megaliths, or lean against them, eyes closed. The blending of ivy and mistletoe, wellies,

---

* The ditch is actually the oldest part of the site, built in 3100 BC.

costumes and Santa hats is utterly charming, sincerity and insincerity swirled together, crowded among the millennia-old stones. The sky is overcast, and no one is really expecting a proper sunrise, but we're all here to experience it nonetheless.

And then just as dawn comes, improbably, impossibly, the clouds part for a moment and golden sunlight spills out. I'm standing right in the centre of Stonehenge, and it floods down to me through an arch in the outer ring, and then another in the centre, framed by two sets of stone doorways. In the cold dawn of midwinter as the sun rises at last after its longest night, there is silence and then joyous cheering, as we let the magic settle over us, let it seep through our skin.

This magic is, in part, the knowledge that the relentless tide of darkness has turned, that light will start to return. It's partly the happiness surrounding me – the earnest cheers and song, the well wishes shouted by strangers in a moment of happy abandon that we're all experiencing together, huddled in the strange circle of stones. But it's also the way that, in the moment of the sun's rising, the vast gulfs of history and understanding that separate us from the builders of Stonehenge seem to vanish. It's so easy to imagine that over five millennia ago people might have stood right where we are standing, looked at the same dawn, the same stones, might have celebrated that they, too, were beginning the long road back out of the winter darkness. There is so much power in that sensation of connection, the feeling of seeing a handprint millennia old and instinctively slipping your own hand over it, of all that time contracting so you and people thousands of years ago are – for a brief instant – the same. You could believe a lot in places and moments like these, destabilised, enchanted, feeling your way through time.

Not all of those beliefs are comforting. There's a darkness in plenty of our stories about ancient pagan practices, a suggestion that they were bound up in violence and sacrifice, that our ancestors worshipped dark gods and trod dark ways. After the sunrise, I slip out from Stonehenge's circle to visit the 'slaughter stone', which lies a few metres away. A long, flat rectangle of rock, the stone is pitted from millennia of exposure to the elements and where the pits have filled with rain the water is a deep, unsettling shade of red. There are stories which whisper that Stonehenge was once a site of horrific sacrifices, of innocents tied down to the slaughter stone, of murderous druids holding aloft golden sickles that glinted in the midwinter sun. In those tellings, the red liquid of the stone is the blood of Stonehenge's victims, built up over millennia, seeping slowly out of the rock. Perhaps five thousand years is as close as I want to come to the original worshippers of Stonehenge after all.

This suggestion of pagan darkness isn't limited to the solstice at Stonehenge. It hangs over all the Christmas traditions described in this book. Krampus is often claimed as an ancient pagan god, on everything from travel sites advertising the Krampus runs to interviews with Krampus performers themselves, and Holda and Perchta are supposedly ancient Germanic goddesses, their processions of the dead a pre-Christian belief in the Wild Hunt rampaging through the skies. Mari Lwyd, meanwhile, is a figure of grinning death representing (according to one folklorist) 'horrific origin and intention'. More terrifyingly still, the Lord of Misrule has been suggested as a half-remembered fertility ritual whose climax was the death of the mock king at the end of the Christmas period – a sacrifice still – supposedly – remembered in the death of the hero in the mummers plays. In fact, the Marshfield Mummers refuse to allow women to participate in their play because of this supposed origin.[*] It lends a new sense of chilling dark magic to all the Christmas monsters – a feeling that by participating in the rituals surrounding them I'm walking the same paths as my ancestors, and that I might find something shadowy and terrifying walking with me.

But all that magic might be clouding my vision, and the modern winter celebrations at Stonehenge are a clear warning of this. Midwinter was certainly enormously important to the builders of Stonehenge – the tallest trilithion (the largest, central arch of stones in the interior

---

[*]   Incidentally, even if you buy into the idea that the play is a half-remembered ancient ritual, the players happily acknowledge that the day of the performance changed from Christmas Day to Boxing Day, that in the late nineteenth century the play was performed by children rather than adults, and claim that the costumes were originally made of leaves rather than paper, so clearly some changes were absolutely fine. And that's before we even get into the fact that the supposed fertility ritual ended with the actual death of the king, so they're not even doing the most crucial part of the entire thing. Start murdering someone annually or let women take part.

semicircle) and the Avenue (the main route into the site) were both set up so that you would walk to Stonehenge directly into the midwinter sun, shining through the arch formed by the most prominent set of stones. But despite the modern festivities taking place at sunrise, Stonehenge is not arranged to mark the dawn at the end of the longest night. Instead, it's aligned with the midwinter sunset, and the end of the shortest day.[*] As I (and four thousand-odd other people) celebrate the dawn on the morning of 22 December, I'm not – despite all the magical sensations – watching the sunrise from the same place as my 'ancestors', and if I were to slip back through time by a few thousand years I wouldn't see Neolithic peoples cheering on the dawn. At most I might see someone prepping for the party to come. I also wouldn't see anyone being sacrificed (at any time of the day, or year) – there's no evidence that sacrifices took place at Stonehenge, or in the rest of the ritual complex surrounding it.[†] The 'blood' of the slaughter stone is caused by the

---

[*]    I did see the sun rise through a gap in the stones, but it was a random one slightly off to the right (if you're standing with your back to the tallest trilithon). Given that Stonehenge is a circle, any sunrise will come through a stone doorway as long as you're standing in the right place (or at least, it would, before some of the stones collapsed).

[†]    Human sacrifice is very difficult to discern in the archaeological record, but there is only one single burial at Stonehenge that it's possible to read as such – a man who was shot at point blank range with arrows, probably by two people. But of course, he could just as easily be a murder victim or an executed criminal (or some overlap between the categories).

iron in the rock and the algae living in the water, and the stone itself would have been upright, rather than lying flat, when Stonehenge was in use. And that should be our first warning as we step into some very murky territory. History built on magic and feeling is never very good history, even if it can be used to tell some good stories.*

As the party among the megaliths begins to wind down, and the horns, wellies and druidic robes are packed away in the car park, I head out across the mud to the east, to a site called Durrington Walls. All there is to see here is the sweeping curve of a low embankment in an empty field, and this morning it's entirely deserted, so quiet and empty after the raucous gathering at Stonehenge that the stillness feels unnerving. In the growing drizzle, with the Salisbury plain stretching away in every direction, it seems the height of desolation.

But once, on midwinter morning, this is where the party was. Durrington Walls is (probably) where the builders of Stonehenge lived and is the site of another circle made of enormous wooden posts, known today as the Southern Circle. Recreations of the Circle show it as a surreal forest of gigantic, bare tree trunks, angular, geometric, full of long, straight lines and long straight

---

* This isn't a criticism of the modern celebrations, which are a delight and serve their own purpose for people who want to embrace the end of the longest night and the way out of winter. Traditions and folklore should shift – that's how they grow.

shadows. And this site, unlike Stonehenge, *was* orientated towards the midwinter sunrise. It was in use at the same time as Stonehenge as well – so perhaps people welcomed the sun in the wood and bid it farewell among the stones.

Excavations at Durrington Walls have given us even more evidence of the midwinter festivities in the distant past – there were, apparently, huge midwinter pork feasts there. Tens of thousands of pig bones were found at the site – still a little blackened from being roasted, still with the cut marks from the butcher, and most of them from animals about seven months old (which, with most animals born is spring, is how we know that they're likely the remains of a midwinter feast). As I stand there, improperly breakfasted and in the bitter damp of a morning that's gone from overcast to drizzling to properly raining, I promise myself sausages when I get home.

It's not just Stonehenge and the sites around it that show us midwinter was important in Northern Europe prior to Christianity. There are plenty of monuments dating from the Neolithic to the Bronze Age which seem to be aligned with either the setting or the rising midwinter sun. There are a few other hints to midwinter celebrations in much later sources as well. We know, for example, that Yule was at least a word being used for winter in the fifth or sixth century AD when it appears on a calendar of month names, and in the eighth century AD the English historian Bede recorded that the Saxon month of '*giuli*' corresponded with either December or January. Bede also, very cryptically, mentioned a night called 'Mōdraniht' or 'mother's night', celebrated by the pagan Saxons on 25 December. Clearly, he had no idea what actually went on then, and he's the only source for this mysterious celebration, making it impossible for us to know anything more about it. Perhaps it was an ancient heathen rite of fertility, but it's also very possible that Bede was confused and it was actually a festival of Christianised Saxons commemorating Mary, who had, after all, become a mother on the night of the 25th. With a single name to go on, recorded by a source who said that he 'suspected' it was called that 'because of the rituals they performed'* you could substitute any number of other guesses. There are also few later literary sources which suggest that the pagan midwinter festivals involved plentiful drinking, feasting and wearing nice clothes (and in some Nordic countries, possibly the swearing of oaths on a 'yule pig', which was then summarily eaten).

And then, finally, there was the playing of the stag, attested as a 1 January tradition in Late Antiquity and seemingly unrelated to either the pagan Roman or Christian festivities – but, as we've seen, it's impossible to know its significance, or how far back it dated. We're making an educated guess when we say it may have come from non-Roman, pre-Christian European midwinter traditions, but if we invent any set of beliefs that might have swirled around it at that time, we're just writing fiction.

---

\*    Thanks, Bede, very helpful, not irritatingly vague at all.

And that is pretty much that for our knowledge of pre-Christian Northern European midwinter celebrations. There are no other sources – no writings have survived from the people themselves, and none of the Roman writers who encountered them ever recorded any (not that much written by the Romans about Northern European cultures can be taken at face value). You might notice that in all of this there is a distinct lack of Krampus-gods, Wild Hunts, sacrificial fertility rites, and ceremonial Christmas murders. In fact, this was probably spoiled for you already by this entire book, which has detailed how most of these traditions appeared, and hasn't mentioned Christmassy murder rituals once. So why do we think that our Christmas monsters are connected to ancient pagan rites?

We probably have to start in the early 1800s with the Brothers Grimm, or at least with one of the brothers, Jacob. As well as collecting and recording fairy tales with his brother Wilhelm, Jacob wrote an enormous tome about the history of Germanic myth. In it, he suggested that hidden within modern folklore were the surviving remnants of pre-Christian faiths, that the epic sagas of once great and powerful religions lived on in nursery tales and fairy stories. It's a beautiful and enticing idea, and you can see it genuinely happening in some cases – there were plenty of eighteenth-century folktales about the Norse god Thor. The problem was that Grimm didn't want to take what we know about Germanic pagan belief and look for it in modern folklore; he wanted to take fairy stories and use them to reconstruct ancient myths, to create the framework of an entire religion from stories being told in the same geographic area about two thousand years later.

He was especially determined that the Christmas witches were once pagan goddesses of winter. In some of the fairy tales Grimm encountered, Holda makes her bed and the flying feathers from the down become snow. This is a fun, fanciful and appropriate bit of storytelling – Holda is domestic and Christmassy, but still magical. Grimm however, claimed that this little vignette shows that Holda was once a goddess of the ancient Germans who created snow and, since 'the Greeks ascribed the production of snow and rain to their Zeus, so Holda comes before us as a goddess of no mean rank' – which is an incredible set of leaps to make. There's a big difference between an eighteenth-century fairy tale telling us that whenever Holda shook out her bedding the feathers became snow and the claim that she was – thousands of years before – a goddess who controlled the weather. And even if you were to buy that (which you absolutely shouldn't), there's no reason why the creation of snow should make a Germanic goddess impressive just because the top god made snow in ancient Greece.[*] And then, of course, there's the fact that Holda only appears in our

---

[*] There is also an independent snow goddess in ancient Greece. She's called Chione, and the reason you haven't heard of her is because she was indeed a very minor figure.

151

sources in the medieval period and there's no reason at all to think that she was someone who might be recognised by an ancient pagan hanging out in the area that is now Germany.

Grimm was also the one who pushed the idea of the 'Wild Hunt' as a pagan survival – he took all the tales of the female figures leading other women or parades of the dead, as well as the related medieval traditions of wandering bands of armies, and claimed that they all had ancient pagan roots and were part of a coherent set of beliefs whereby either a pagan goddess or Odin himself had once led the troop through the night. This isn't true – we've seen how these stories developed – but it didn't stop the idea taking hold.* And while Grimm's focus was mainly on the Christmas witches – he casually suggests Knecht Ruprecht started out as a 'helper-elf or kobold' in ancient pagan belief – the other Christmas monsters would be dragged into it all soon enough, because in 1890 James Frazer came along and wrote the *The Golden Bough: A Study in Magic and Religion*, a book all about supposedly murderous pagan traditions.

Frazer firmly reinforced Grimm's ideas of pagan survivals, writing in his introduction that:

---

* We don't – alas – have time to get into all the exciting ins and outs of the Wild Hunt mythos without making this book entirely Wild Hunt focused, with me occasionally popping to Salzburg to see a Krampus or two. But if you are interested, then Ronald Hutton's 2014 article *The Wild Hunt and the Witches' Sabbath* is open access and available for free online.

The great intellectual and moral forces which have revolutionised the educated world have scarcely affected the peasant. In his inmost beliefs he is what his forefathers were in the days when forest trees still grew and squirrels played on the ground where Rome and London now stand.[1]

Here, the 'peasant' is someone who still holds and practises ancient beliefs, never changing them, never adding to them, having had them passed to him by his similarly unimaginative ancestors for thousands of years. If you're beginning to think that sounds like a bit of a stretch, and that Frazer might have some views on 'peasantry' that he could do with looking at a second time, you'd be right. In fact, Frazer's entire book is a collection of wild, unsubstantiated statements with some vaguely unpleasant notions of 'common' and 'primitive' men mixed in.

But Frazer also had one very specific idea to add to Grimm's theories. He thought that all ancient religions were fertility cults and revolved around electing a sacred king and then sacrificing him. A new ruler would then take up the mantel of kingship – a symbolic 'reviving' that mirrored the death and revival of nature. According to Frazer this went on left, right and centre, in multiple religions and across the world,[*] and one of his many 'examples' of

---

[*]  Including in Christianity – for Frazer, the story of the sacrificed and revived Jesus was another example of this, a theory that got him into plenty of trouble, to the extent that he removed the idea entirely from his later abridged edition.

it happening was the Lord of Misrule and Saturnalia celebrations which, he claimed, actually involved the mock king elected for the festival being murdered.

His evidence for this was a fourth-century text which described how a Christian – Dasius – was executed for refusing to take on the role of king at Saturnalia which, according to this single source, would have involved Dasius being sacrificed to a pagan god. The historian who originally published the text (and most people afterwards), generally think that the author was confused, and that Dasius would have needed to *make* a sacrifice to a pagan god, not *been* sacrificed himself.* The author was after all, a Christian himself, and perhaps didn't fully understand the ceremony (not to mention that it didn't harm the Christian cause to make other religions look as barbaric as possible). And, of course, we have plentiful accounts of Saturnalia, and the election of mock kings, and only this one late, confused suggestion of human sacrifice. Nero was elected king of Saturnalia and certainly survived it all, and Pliny might have felt he needed more than a well soundproofed suite of rooms if the 'holiday freedoms' of the rest of the household involved someone being murdered.†

---

\* Very much a 'how to cook people'/'how to cook for people' situation.

† To be fair to Frazer, he did suggest that the Romans themselves were 'civilised' people, and that their Saturnalia no longer involved the sacrifice – but surely the Romans would have commented if people around them were practising that same celebration – and murdering someone during it.

But *The Golden Bough* was written for the general audience, and proved to be immensely popular.* It didn't seem to matter much that plenty of academics weren't impressed by Frazer's theories when his book brought the idea of pagan survivals much more vividly, and more poetically, to people's attention than Grimm had ever done. He describes, in lyrical, beautiful prose, sacred groves and the murderous priests who stalk them, opening his book on the:

> dream-like vision of the little woodland lake of Nemi – 'Diana's Mirror,' as it was called by the ancients. No one who has seen that calm water, lapped in a green hollow of the Alban hills, can ever forget it. The two characteristic Italian villages which slumber on its banks, and the equally Italian palace whose terraced gardens descend steeply to the lake, hardly break the stillness and even the solitariness of the scene. Diana herself might still linger by this lonely shore, still haunt these woodlands wild.[2]

His telling is seductive in its loveliness, a bright beauty enhanced by the thrilling current of danger and death that stalks through his ancient trees. Are the 'peasants'

---

* Unlike Grimm's *German Mythologies*, which, by the third sentence, is digging into the nominative singular terminations of the word 'God' in various Germanic languages. By the fourth sentence, he's into irregular genitives and there's no coming back.

in touch with the old ways and living in a pre-industrial utopia, or are they terrifying savages? In Frazer's vision, they're somehow both. Even knowing that it's all nonsense, you can see why its vision so beguiled people when it first appeared.

The only bit of Christmas folklore Frazer mentioned was the Lord of Misrule, but it didn't take long for people to start suggesting more examples of modern-day survivals of ancient Christmas sacrifices. The first to go were the mummers plays. With the play revolving around the death and resurrection of the central character, folklorists started claiming that it was a corrupted re-enactment of the sacrifice of the Christmas King. It didn't bother any of them that there were no attestations of the death and resurrection play prior to the eighteenth century – after all, according to Frazer and Grimm the peasants hadn't changed their ways for millennia. If common people were doing it, and it wasn't explicitly Christian, then it just had to be a millennia-old tradition.

Slowly, the idea of pagan survivals started to creep into everything. 'The running of the deer' in 'The Holly and the Ivy' was a surviving reference to a pre-historic deer cult – despite the fact that the song can only be traced back to the early nineteenth century. A Stone Age painting of a horse was a clear reference to the guising, snapping horse monsters of the UK – despite thousands of years separating them.* Santa, meanwhile, was in fact

---

* And look, even if there *had* been horse guising going on when the painting was made, there's no reason to believe that any and every

Odin himself and his eight reindeer a shifted vision of his eight-legged horse Sleipnir – he's not, of course, we've seen how St Nicholas's legends developed, and Odin isn't involved at any point. (In fact, we can actually track the addition of the reindeer to Santa's mythos to one author – Clement Clark Moore – who wrote a book called *A Visit from St Nicholas* in 1822 and decided to include a team of reindeer. If Moore was thinking of Odin when he did so, he didn't happen to mention it.) Krampus barely appears in *German Mythologies*, but the monster couldn't stay out of the fray for long and soon he was a pagan god, an 'anonymous Grand Master roaring in the ecstasy of Divine possession', his chains and birch rod 'a remnant of pagan initiation rites'[3] (did these rites involve fertility and death? Of course they did). The ideas became wilder and wilder, the connections more and more tenuous, and the writing describing it more and more flowery.*

---

      painting of a horse was referencing it. After all, at the highest period of horse-guising Christmas popularity in England, there were still plenty of images of horses knocking about that had absolutely nothing to do with guising.

\*     One of my absolute favourite accounts of this comes from Kirby, an American scholar working in the 1970s. He wrote crossly that of course mummers plays and Christmas monsters weren't ancient fertility or initiation rituals, and goes into all the sensible reasons to explain why they aren't. It's a practical, reasoned argument, until two pages in when he claims that it's in fact obvious that it was an ancient *shamanic* healing rite that started everything. It's like watching someone state all the very clear reasons why the belief in a flat earth is nonsense, only for their conclusion to be that it's actually a cylinder.

There are, of course, innumerable issues with all of this – the main one being that the foundation of Grimm and Frazer's ideas is that 'Culture' and 'Tradition' are serious, that they are invented by the upper classes, and given to the lower, who can only continue to slavishly repeat the rites and rituals they've been handed, even if they forget the meaning behind it all without their social betters to remind them. It doesn't allow for anyone from the 'peasantry' to create a new legend, or a new celebration, or a new monster. Instead, every single story has to be a half-remembered variant of an ancient myth or god. It is an extraordinary vision of folklore, one that is almost entirely static, entirely freed from imagination – except thousands of years ago, when people invented all legends and folklore and then immediately stopped. And as we've seen with Christmas monsters, while threads of folklore can stretch back for millennia, it is still, overwhelmingly, wild and creative, bringing mayhem in its wake, constantly evolving and changing, adding new bits and abandoning others. And while everyone, from every social class, indulged in dark Christmas traditions, it's the people Frazer decided were 'peasants' and refused to credit with any creativity at all who were responsible for huge parts of the invention of monstrous Christmas folklore.

It's notable as well that all these ideas of ancient pagan rituals don't allow our ancestors to have any fun. Electing a Lord of Misrule can only have been a solemn ritual, rather than an enjoyable piece of slightly unsettling 'scandalous stupidity'. Krampus must have been revered and genuinely feared – he can't just have been a monster used to give everyone a thrilling little fright. There might be some seriousness underpinning the Christmas horrors – it's certainly true that midwinter must once have been genuinely terrifying, a period of piercing cold and all-encompassing darkness that could not be kept at bay, that might not even be survivable. The Christmas monsters could have been a way of realising this fear, of turning it into something that – though still terrifying – could be controlled, even defeated. But while this may be part of the reason for our Christmas hauntings, it's certainly not the only one. It's often said that Christmas is a celebration of the light – a way of driving out the darkness of midwinter, but I think we want to celebrate the darkness as well, to plunge ourselves into it, use it to make things as excitingly horrifying as they can be, to fill the night with monsters and scares that take full advantage of the longer, deeper darkness, and enjoy all the terrifying possibilities it brings, knowing deep down that it's a horror of our own making, and can be – just about – controlled. This is horror as entertainment – horror to be relished. There's too much fun in the monsters for them to be solely representations of a genuine fear, too much joy taken in the subversive excitement of rampaging through the night, whether as a witch, Krampus or snapping monster, too much laughter mingling with the screams that echo through the centuries.

No one we meet in the sources was electing a king of Saturnalia because of some intense, ancient religious belief – it was only ever some nonsense, done to enhance the wildness and abandon of the season. No one ever seems to be guising for deeply serious beliefs either – it all seems to be enjoyable, a bit of a scare, a licence to be wild for the night. What sets apart the Christmas witches (and to some extent the Christmas werewolves) is that for a few hundred years one group of powerful people with vested interests did start to take them seriously, with violent consequences – but in this they are unique among the Christmas monsters, and the emergence of the witch hunts had very little to do with the celebration of Christmas (in fact, Christmas was quickly filtered out of the witch trials, as if everyone was aware that it gave the whole thing a slightly un-serious air). No one was ever hunting a Mari Lwyd or a Krampus – except some authorities desperately trying to stop the very human guisers from running amok. There might be some violence (even death) bound up in letting social rules slip away, in filling the world with chaos – but it's all in understandable, human terms, not people solemnly sacrificing to their dark and terrible gods.

Chrysologos, complaining about Kalends, claimed that his congregation would insist to him that the Kalends celebrations:

> are just for fun; this is a celebration of a new beginning ... this is just New Year.[4]

He clearly didn't believe them, but after immersing myself in Christmas darkness, I'm inclined to take their statements at face value. I have rarely had as much fun as I've had being chased by Krampuses, or frightened by

mummers, or holding Twelfth Night parties and electing
Queens of Christmas.

And yet, despite knowing all of this, I'm surprised to find
that a part of me wants the stories of the nineteenth-
and twentieth-century folklorists to be true. While I'm
celebrating at Stonehenge, I see a giant black goat, mingling with the crowd, wearing a crown of ivy and roses.
He catches me off guard – he looks, for all the world, like
a Krampus prowling among the stones, blending with
their lost, old magic, even if, when I get closer, I see that
it's a man in robes, a goat head perched on top of his
own like a hat.* It's all very well saying that Krampus –
as we would recognise him – appeared in the eighteenth
and nineteenth centuries, but don't we all secretly want
him to be a long lost god, horns twined with holly and
ivy, stalking through a silent, snowy grove, the air heavy
with the scent of moss and dread, leading us somewhere darker, somewhere more exciting, than we could
imagine? Don't we want the magic to be real?†

There so many good layers to the theories of the nineteenth century folklorists – the poetry of a tradition

---

\*    I long to ask him why he's wearing it, what string of folklore he's
pulling on, but he's bent in silent prayer, his hand on one of the
megaliths, and even I'm not obnoxious enough to interrupt.

†    I know, as well, that part of me is glad that Krampus's horns can be
traced back to Late Antiquity, and maybe further – that they might
emerge from the darkness of a pre-Christian midwinter.

preserved for millennia, handed down through time until its meaning is lost but its practice is still recognisable, of ancient and important rites crushed by the bigotry of Christianity until they are only visible through cryptic community rituals. It's a story, too, of connection with the land, with history, an idea that the 'common folk' were still tied to our ancient past, to a time when London was a forest – an idea that resonated as Europe became increasingly urbanised, as people felt like they were losing their roots, and resonates still.

And that, of course, is why these ideas stuck – they're very good stories. In fact, many of the folklorists were writing them more as fiction than theories. Violet Alford, famed for her work on the mummers plays (and the folklorist who restarted the Marshfield Mummers, while assuring the participants that it was an ancient fertility ritual) said that, when it came to folklore:

> It does seem to me that imagination is needed. On the vision evoked facts can be built, and pulled down again if they do not fit.[5]

You can't build history on the foundation of imagination with some facts balanced precariously on top (let alone if you're pulling the facts down if they don't fit the vision), but it is a good way of writing some very enticing fictions. And it was often artists who took up the mantel. Sixty years after Frazer's *Golden Bough*, the poet Robert Graves wrote *The White Goddess*, a book entirely made up of delightful nonsense about pagan rituals and asserting that the death-and-resurrection mummers plays were 'the clearest survivals of the pre-Christian religion'. This in turn inspired Sylvia Plath, who found herself identifying with Grave's goddess – a sister of Holda – who he put at the centre of it all. It inspired books like Susan Cooper's *The Dark Is Rising*, the children's story from 1973 about the dark, pagan magic that bleeds through into Christmas and midwinter. Plenty of our most beloved horror stories are based on these ideas too, from *The Wicker Man* to *Midsommar* and, arguably, the entire genre of folk horror.

This idea of pagan darkness is often not treated like an academic theory, but more like a new bit of folklore, a new addition to the myths of the Christmas monsters. The stories of ancient pagan sacrifices at midwinter are told with a breathless and excited terror, a way of lending fear and importance to the traditions. And while it isn't true that the monsters are the survivals of ancient, blood-soaked rites, it's also not true that Krampus steals away misbehaving children, or that Perchta flies through the night with the dead. But both stories are told, both with the same glint in the teller's eye at the idea of darkness and fear, irrespective of truth. Because that's what happens with folklore – it's one of the most incredible things about it. It is so mutable (and so discerning) that to touch it is to change it, and to touch it with a good story, with an extra, repeatable, understandable new dimension, is to rework it entirely. It doesn't matter, not even for one moment, what is right and correct – it only matters what's fun and interesting. And Krampus as a pagan god, the mummers plays as ancient sacrificial rituals – are definitely that. It's delightfully ironic that folklore is so dynamic that it happily absorbed a story about it being entirely static and unchanging just because it happened to be a very *good* story.

And these new ideas did something else as well – they made the Christmas monsters frightening again, just at a time when the darker side of Christmas practices were, to some extent, dying out. The folklorists of the nineteenth and twentieth centuries were often recording the very last iterations of these traditions (some of the mummers plays variants were narrated by the last person alive to have seen them enacted). There are plenty of reasons for this – not least the arrival of the new, family-centred, non-chaotic Victorian Christmas. But it might not be a coincidence that these practices were also fading as beliefs in demons, witches and devils were disappearing almost entirely, as the ghost stories they told lost some of the final vestiges of their power. It's telling as well that they started to come back with a vengeance when folklorists created a new set of horror stories for them – ones that were genuinely believable again. To people who were unlikely to believe in a real demon, the idea that Krampus carried with him millennia of bloody death allowed him to retain a huge portion of the exciting terror he might otherwise have lost.

I'd be lying if I said that this extra layer of horror doesn't haunt me now at Christmas, as much as the other ghosts. In the same way that I might have gone on the Year Walk a firm unbeliever in the power of magic but was still afraid of what I might see, I went to mummers plays and dark Christmas ceremonies knowing full well that there was no truth to the idea of pagan sacrifices, let alone ones still practised today. But I still knew what happens in stories to outsiders intruding on long-forgotten rituals,* and there was still a nagging unease at the back of my mind. What if, in some alpine town lost in the snow, or a village buried deep in the English countryside, the Old Ways haven't been forgotten? What if that town or village is the very same one where I happen to be watching a Krampus run or mummers play right now? Is that Krampus performer growling at me truly just playing? Are the mummers clacking their blades a little too violently? *Am I sure I'm entirely safe?*

---

* And that the ones intruding to 'study' the rituals, or, god forbid, write a book about them, tend – quite rightly – to come out the worst of all.

# The Dead of Winter

*Christmas Day*

It's the evening of Christmas Day. I'm curled up in an armchair under the soft, golden light of the Christmas tree, sunk in the exhausted happiness that comes after a day of celebration and excitement. The house is quiet, suffused with the smell of the tree, the brandy from the burning of the Christmas pudding, the hot spice and oranges of a mulled wine that's simmering on the stove, an array of scents that recall every Christmas past, every Christmas evening spent curled up just like this. Everything in the room seems to be gently sparkling: not just the fairy lights and baubles, but the glinting scrap of wrapping paper on the floor, the golden candle-holder on the table, the foil on the little pile of chocolate boxes, the lettering on the spines of my new, Christmas-gifted books. I am in a world of bright enchantment and peace, and in my hands is my tattered, much-beloved copy of M. R. James's *Ghost Stories of An Antiquary*.

Reading a Victorian ghost story every Christmas is the dark Christmas tradition that I've observed since I was a child, so that even with a stocking at the end of my bed and a glittering tree downstairs my head was filled with images of a ghastly withered hand reaching out over an ancient manuscript, or monsters summoned by an antique whistle to haunt grey and lonely beaches. Written in the late eighteenth and early nineteenth centuries, M. R. James created his stories to be read aloud on Christmas Eve, and he was far from the only Victorian author making ghostly tales for the season. There was James Skipp Borlase, who took pre-existing ghost stories and reworked them (badly) so they took place at Christmas. Henry James's *The Turn of the Screw* had his tale of a governess in a haunted mansion being read aloud on Christmas Eve, to a group of friends gathered around a fire, and Jerome K. Jerome used the telling of Christmas Eve ghost stories as a framing device for his 1891 ghost-story collection, *Told After Supper*, claiming in his introduction that:

> Whenever five or six English-speaking people meet round a fire on Christmas Eve, they start telling each other ghost stories ... It is a genial, festive season, and we love to muse upon graves, and dead bodies, and murders, and blood.[1]

Washington Irving, in his book of Christmas traditions, *Old Christmas*, also remembered the telling of ghost
stories – in his case, about a ghostly Crusading knight – at
Christmas. Even Dickens, advocating so influentially for
the more wholesome Christmas, did so through a ghost
story in *A Christmas Carol*.

Like the folklorists spinning beguiling fantasies of
ancient pagan rituals, Jerome, Borlase, Dickens and the
Jameses (M.R. and Henry) were tapping into the old need
for darkness within the new, Victorian, family Christmas,
when people were meant to be getting cosy round the
tree or roasting chestnuts by the fire with their nearest
and dearest, and not rampaging drunkenly through the
streets in a horrible mask. The traditions might have
shifted, and the tales may have been rendered in a form
that could be enjoyed quietly, at home, with your family,
but everyone still wanted midwinter to be full of ghosts
and monsters.

And we seem to want it even more now: we're living
in a new boom period for Christmas monsters. Krampus
runs, Mari Lwyd wassails and mummers plays are all
seeing record attendances. Krampus runs have even
spread to the US, appearing everywhere from Portland
to Dallas, to LA (which can only lead to worries that the
shagged, furred outfits built for running in the Alpine
snow were perhaps not made for a December with an
average temperature of 20 degrees). Covid staggered the
rise of these monsters to some extent (the Chepstow
Wassail I attended was the first one since 2019), but it's
starting to look like this was a temporary blip. Despite

familial obligations,* despite the difficulty in travelling over Christmas, every dark Christmas celebration I encountered was thoroughly packed out.

Some of this modern embrace of the darker side of Christmas may be a pushback against the saccharine nature of our celebrations – an antidote to the cloyingly twee commercialisation that so many feel the festivities now represent. It's impossible as well to look away from the fact that some people embracing our Christmas monsters are doing so because they feel it allows them to wear blackface, or exclude women, in a way they might not be able to get away with if they weren't claiming it was for 'tradition's' sake – a last refuge for people who think a bit of racism and misogyny is some much needed Christmas spice.† I wonder too if, as we lose our winters to the warming climate, we like the idea of Christmas monsters whose coming emphasises the changing of the season in a way that the weather might not.

And of course, the horror helps to emphasise the other side of Christmas – the roaring fires, the good company and good food, made even warmer and brighter by contrasting them with the chill of ghosts and hauntings.

---

* In case you're wondering, writing a book on ghostly Christmas traditions can get you out of some of the familial obligations, so you can pop to mummers plays on Boxing Day and Krampus runs on the only December weekend that everyone's free for the family party, but you'll be in for double the following year.

† If they genuinely cared about tradition, they'd be embracing the period as a time when gender was erased and social orders flipped, but they always seem happy to ignore that part.

As I sit in my armchair on Christmas evening, I know that my warm little circle of golden light feels so much more precious with the night outside – and with Krampus prowling through the darkness while Perchta and her dead fly overhead, while knives are being sharpened for another round of mummers-day murderers tomorrow. It's little wonder that the monsters survived the Victorianisation of Christmas when they could make the comforts of home and family feel so much more powerful. And the family-based Christmas draws ghosts near in other ways as well. Christmas is the time when I feel most keenly the absence of the people I have lost and the people I am losing, but also when I feel closest to them. It's when, sitting in my chair on Christmas Day, I can almost imagine that my father is sitting reading with me, as he did on so many Christmas evenings, about to read aloud a passage from his book that he thinks will interest me, to talk with me about it late into the night. It's when a slice of Christmas cake brings the taste of those my grandmother made (baked in November and fed through the weeks until they were so sodden with alcohol they almost dripped, mishappen by the baking sheet, cracked, burnt, dark, delicious). Those who are gone, those who are leaving us, draw close again at Christmas, whether passing through in Perchta's hunt, attending ghostly churches on Christmas Eve or conjured by our memories, and we reach out to them.

# Notes

ONE: Lords of Misrule

1. Pliny, Letters 2, XVII, 24.
2. Seneca. *Letters on Ethics: To Lucilius*. Chicago: University of Chicago Press, 2015, 67.
3. Suetonius, The Life of Augustus, 75.
4. Lucian, *The Works of Lucian of Samosata* Vol. 4. Oxford: Clarendon, 190.
5. Justinus, Epitome of Pompeius Trogus, 43.3.
6. Lucian, *The Works of Lucian of Samosata* Vol. 4. Oxford: Clarendon, 190.
7. Max Harris, *Sacred Folly: A New History of the Feast of Fools*. Ithaca: Cornell University Press, 2011, 27.
8. Max Harris, *Sacred Folly: A New History of the Feast of Fools*. Ithaca: Cornell University Press, 2011, 29.
9. Max Harris, *Sacred Folly: A New History of the Feast of Fools*. Ithaca: Cornell University Press, 2011, 31.
10. Max Harris, 'Claiming Pagan Origins for the Carnival: Bacchanalia, Saturnalia and Kalends', *European Medieval Drama* Vol. 10, 86.

11.  Max Harris, *Sacred Folly: A New History of the Feast of Fools*. Ithaca: Cornell University Press, 2011, 106.
12.  Max Harris, *Sacred Folly: A New History of the Feast of Fools*. Ithaca: Cornell University Press, 2011, 16.
13.  Ronald Hutton, *The Stations of the Sun: A History of the Ritual Year in Britain*. Oxford: Oxford University Press, 1996, 123.
14.  Al Ridenour, *The Krampus and the Old, Dark Christmas: Roots and Rebirth of the Folkloric Devil*. Minneapolis: Feral House, 2016, 120.
15.  Phillip Stubbes *Anatomie of Abuses in England*. London, 1583, 148.
16.  Increase Mather, *A Testimony Against Several Prophane and Superstitious Customs*. London, 1687, 3.7.
17.  Phillip Stubbes, *Anatomie of Abuses in England*. London, 1583, 147.
18.  Max Harris, 'Claiming Pagan Origins for the Carnival: Bacchanalia, Saturnalia and Kalends', *European Medieval Drama* Vol. 10, 104.

## TWO: Monstrous Visitors

1.  Ioana Repciuc, 'A New Perspective on the Old Documents Concerning the Analysis of Animal Folk Masquerade'. *Clasic și modern în cercetarea filologică românească actuală*, 2019, 461.
2.  Al Ridenour, *The Krampus and the Old, Dark Christmas: Roots and Rebirth of the Folkloric Devil*. Minneapolis: Feral House, 2016, 122. (Though Ridenour claims that this was written by the Archbishop of Canterbury in the 7th century – it wasn't. It was a clause added to the Archbishop's penitential in France or Germany a couple of centuries later – something discussed at the end of the Horse Skulls and Hoodenings chapter.)
3.  Max Harris, 'Claiming Pagan Origins for the Carnival:

Bacchanalia, Saturnalia and Kalends', *European Medieval Drama* Vol. 10, 84.

4.   Max Harris, 'Claiming Pagan Origins for the Carnival: Bacchanalia, Saturnalia and Kalends', *European Medieval Drama* Vol. 10, 84.

5.   Max Harris, *Sacred Folly: A New History of the Feast of Fools*. Ithaca: Cornell University Press, 2011, 31.

6.   Max Harris, 'Claiming Pagan Origins for the Carnival: Bacchanalia, Saturnalia and Kalends', *European Medieval Drama* Vol. 10, 89.

7.   Terry Gunnell, 'Gryla, Grylur, Groleks and Skeklers', *Nordic Yearbook of Folklore* vol. 57, 2001, 42.

8.   Al Ridenour, *The Krampus and the Old, Dark Christmas: Roots and Rebirth of the Folkloric Devil*. Minneapolis: Feral House, 2016, 190.

9.   Derek Schofield, 'Christmas at Uttoxeter: The Guisers Made Their Usual Tour', *Folk Drama Studies Today – International Traditional Drama Conference*, 2002, 24.

## THREE: Horse Skulls and Hoodenings

1.   Rhiannon Ifans, *Stars and Ribbons*, University of Wales Press, 2022, 106.

2.   Rhiannon Ifans, *Stars and Ribbons*, University of Wales Press, 2022, 123.

3.   Rhiannon Ifans, *Stars and Ribbons*, University of Wales Press, 2022, 128.

4.   James Frost, *Animal Guising and the Kentish Hooden Horse*, Ozaru Books, 2023, 7.

## FIVE: The Christmas Witches

1.   *Witchcraft in Europe, 400–1700: A Documentary History*, Alan Charles Kors, Edward Peters (eds). Pennsylvania: University of Pennsylvania Press, 2001, 65.

2.  *Witchcraft in Europe, 400-1700: A Documentary History*, Alan Charles Kors, Edward Peters (eds). Pennsylvania: University of Pennsylvania Press, 2001, 66.
3.  Thomas Leek, 'Holda: Between folklore and linguistics'. *Indogermanische Forschungen*, vol. 113, 2008, 316.
4.  Olaus Magnus, The History of the Northern Peoples, 1555.

## SIX: Old Gods

1.  James Frazer, *The Golden Bough: A Study in Magic and Religion*. Macmillan: 1911, xii.
2.  James Frazer, *The Golden Bough: A Study in Magic and Religion*. London: Macmillan: 1911, 1.
3.  Maurice Bruce, 'The Krampus in Styria' *Folklore*, Vol. 69, No. 1, 1958, 47.
4.  Max Harris, *Sacred Folly: A New History of the Feast of Fools*. Ithaca: Cornell University Press, 2011, 30.
5.  Ronald Hutton, *The Stations of the Sun: A History of the Ritual Year in Britain*. Oxford: Oxford University Press, 1996, 101.

## EPILOGUE: The Dead of Winter

1.  Jerome K. Jerome, *Told After Supper* (1891, London), 16.

# Select Bibliography

This is a short book, and there is so much in the way of dark Christmas traditions that there wasn't space to include. Do go and read everything you can – it's all phenomenally interesting – especially Al Ridenour's *The Krampus and the Old, Dark Christmas*, and Ronald Hutton's *Stations of the Sun*.

B. af Klintberg, *The Types of the Swedish Folk Legend*. Helsinki: Academia Scieniarum Fennica (Folklore Fellowship Communications, 300), 2010.

Tommy Kuusela, '"He Met His Own Funeral Procession": The Year Walk Ritual in Swedish Folk Tradition', in *Folk Belief and Traditions of the Supernatural*, edited by Tommy Kuusela & Giuseppe Maiello. Hong Kong: Beewolf Press, 2016.

*The Dead of Winter*

Al Ridenour, *The Krampus and the Old, Dark Christmas: Roots and Rebirth of the Folkloric Devil*. Minneapolis: Feral House, 2016.

ONE: Lords of Misrule

Fanny Dolansky, 'Celebrating the Saturnalia: Religious Ritual and Roman Domestic Life', *A Companion to Families in the Greek and Roman Worlds*, Beryl Rawson (ed.). St Maldan: Wiley-Blackwell, 2010.

Max Harris, 'Claiming Pagan Origins for the Carnival: Bacchanalia, Saturnalia and Kalends', *European Medieval Drama* 10, 2008.

Max Harris, *Sacred Folly: A New History of the Feast of Fools*. Ithaca: Cornell University Press, 2011.

Ronald Hutton, *The Stations of the Sun: A History of the Ritual Year in Britain*. Oxford: Oxford University Press, 1996.

Al Ridenour, *The Krampus and the Old, Dark Christmas: Roots and Rebirth of the Folkloric Devil*. Minneapolis: Feral House, 2016.

Shulamith Shahar, 'The Boy Bishop's Feast: A Case-study in Church Attitudes towards Children in the High and Late Middle Ages', Diana Wood (ed.), *The Church and Childhood. Studies in Church History* 31, 1994.

**TWO:** Monstrous Visitors

E. C. Cawte, *Ritual Animal Disguise*. London: D. S. Brewer, 1977.

E. K. Chambers, *The Medieval Stage*. 2 Vols. Oxford: Oxford University Press, 1903.

Terry Gunnell, 'Gryla, Grylur, Groleks and Skeklers', *Nordic Yearbook of Folklore* 57, 2001.

Ronald Hutton, *The Stations of the Sun: A History of the Ritual Year in Britain*. Oxford: Oxford University Press, 1996.

Al Ridenour, *The Krampus and the Old, Dark Christmas: Roots and Rebirth of the Folkloric Devil*. Minneapolis: Feral House, 2016.

Meg Twycross and Sarah Carpenter, *Masks and Masking in Medieval and Early Tudor England*. Burlington: Ashgate, 2002.

**THREE:** Horse Skulls and Hoodenings

John Clark '"Playing the stag" in Medieval Middlesex? A perforated antler from South Mimms Castle – parallels and possibilities', K. Baker, R. Carden & R. Madgwick (eds), *Deer and People*. Oxford: Windgather Press, 2015.

George Frampton, *Discordant Comicals: The Hooden Horse of East Kent*. Birchington: Ozaru Books, 2018.

James Frost, *Animal Guising and the Kentish Hooden Horse*. Birchington: Ozaru Books, 2023.

Ronald Hutton, *The Stations of the Sun: A History of the Ritual Year in Britain*. Oxford: Oxford University Press, 1996.

Rhiannon Ifans, *Stars and Ribbons*. Cardiff: University of Wales Press, 2022.

Ioana Repciuc, 'A New Perspective on the Old Documents Concerning the Analysis of Animal Folk Masquerade', *Clasic și modern în cercetarea filologică românească actuală*, Romania: Editura Universității 'Alexandru Ioan Cuza', 2018.

Al Ridenour, *The Krampus and the Old, Dark Christmas: Roots and Rebirth of the Folkloric Devil*. Minneapolis: Feral House, 2016.

FOUR: Punishing the Wicked

Joel Fredell, 'The Three Clerks and St Nicholas in Medieval England', *Studies in Philology*, Vol. 92, No. 2, 1995.

Matthäus Rest and Gertraud Seiser, 'The Krampus in Austria: A Case of Booming Identity Politics',

*EthnoScripts: Zeitschrift für aktuelle ethnologische Studien*, 2018.

Al Ridenour, *The Krampus and the Old, Dark Christmas: Roots and Rebirth of the Folkloric Devil*. Minneapolis: Feral House, 2016.

Marina Warner, *No Go the Bogeyman: Scaring, Lulling, and Making Mock*. London: Chatto & Windus, 1998.

Eric Zafran, 'Saturn and the Jews', *Journal of the Warburg and Courtauld Institutes*. Vol. 42, 1979.

FIVE: The Christmas Witches

Richard Firth Green, *Elf Queens and Holy Friars: Fairy Beliefs and the Medieval Church*. Pennsylvania: University of Pennsylvania Press, 2018.

Ronald Hutton, *Queens of the Wild: Pagan Goddesses in Christian Europe, An Investigation*. New Haven and London: Yale University Press, 2022.

Ronald Hutton, 'The Wild Hunt and the Witches Sabbath', *Folklore* 125, 2018.

Ronald Hutton, *The Witch: A History of Fear, From Ancient Times to the Present*. New Haven and London: Yale University Press, 2017.

Claude Lecourteux, *Phantom Armies of the Night: The Wild Hunt and Ghostly Processions of the Undead*. Toronto: Inner Traditions, 2011.

Al Ridenour, *The Krampus and the Old, Dark Christmas: Roots and Rebirth of the Folkloric Devil*. Minneapolis: Feral House, 2016.

John B. Smith, 'Perchta the Belly-Slitter and Her Kin: A View of Some Traditional Threatening Figures, Threats and Punishments', *Folklore*, Vol. 115, No. 2 (2004).

Emma Wilby, 'Burchard's Strigae, the Witches' Sabbath and Shamanistic Cannibalism in Early Modern Europe', *Magic Ritual and Witchcraft*, Vol. 8, 2018.

*Witchcraft in Europe, 400–1700: A Documentary History*, edited by Alan Charles Kors, Edward Peters. Pennsylvania: University of Pennsylvania Press, 2001.

## SIX: Old Gods

E. K. Chambers, *The Medieval Stage*. 2 Vols. Oxford: Oxford University Press, 1903.

James Frazer, *The Golden Bough: A Study in Magic and Religion*. London: Macmillan, 1911.

Ronald Hutton, *Queens of the Wild: Pagan Goddesses*

*in Christian Europe, An Investigation*, New Haven and London: Yale University Press, 2022.

Ronald Hutton, *The Stations of the Sun: A History of the Ritual Year in Britain*. Oxford: Oxford University Press, 1996.

Mike Pitts, *How to Build Stonehenge*. London: Thames and Hudson, 2022.

## EPILOGUE: The Dead of Winter

I'm only adding a selected title for the epilogue so I can tell you that, although I like my old, tattered edition of *Ghost Stories of An Antiquary*, the best collected M. R. James is the 2011 Oxford World Classics edition. It's one of the few with 'A School Story' and 'The Rose Garden' along with all the obvious choices.

# Acknowledgements

*With enormous thanks*

To Laura, my editor, for all her help, support and incredible suggestions, and to the entire, wonderful team at Granta. To Hayley, my agent, for everything she's done (not least, suggesting that I make this book much more of a travelogue, leading to one of the most incredible Christmas seasons I've ever had). To Mina, for all her help. To Evan, for all his kindness and enthusiasm in making the US edition. To Micaela Alcaino, who designed this book's amazing cover. To Till, Elina, Eeri, Oivi and Aike, for opening your home to me (and teaching me how to make Christmas pastries), to Davide for all his advice about Venice Carnival, and to absolutely everyone who shared their Christmas traditions with me, in any capacity.

To John, for arguing with me about mummers plays and Chambers for months on end, to Annick for making sure we didn't do that for every minute of Christmas. To my mother, for putting up with all my nonsense, to my father, to whom I owe so much of my love for history. To Anne and Gary, with apologies for not seeing you for so much of the Christmas season (and with a promise that I'll make it next year). To Dot, for all her support and kindness. To Afy, Danni and Georgia for being the most wonderful people and friends imaginable. To Danni, Afy, Richard, Michael and Max for having a Twelfth Night party with me, even if you did all make it so very lovely that it would never have fitted into a book about creepy, dark Christmases. And to Max – who has heard every word of this read aloud to him, repeatedly, to the extent that he could probably recite the entire book, who came with me on so many of my Christmas adventures, and who is the main reason my little circle of golden light under the Christmas tree is so full of contentment and happiness.

## IMAGE CREDITS

p. x author's own; p. 10 Venice Carnaval_Venise_4 – Oxxo/Wikimedia Commons; p. 38 author's own; p. 64 author's own; p. 88 author's own; p. 114 Lucia-13.12.06 Claudia Gründer/Wikimedia Commons; p. 140 Storm Clouds Over Stonehenge, Joda Images/Wikimedia Commons; p. 166 from Washington Irving's *Christmas Stories* 1916, Frank Dadd/Wikimedia Commons

# Index

187